College Boards of Trustees

THE LIBRARY OF EDUCATION

A Project of The Center for Applied Research in Education, Inc.

G. R. Gottschalk, Director

Categories of Coverage

I	II	III
Curriculum and Teaching	Administration, Organization, and Finance	Psychology

IV	V	VI
History, Philosophy, and Social Foundations	Professional Skills	Educational Institutions

College Boards of Trustees

S. V. MARTORANA

Director, Office of Planning in
Higher Education
New York State Education Department

1963

The Center for Applied Research in Education, Inc.
Washington, D.C.

Foreword

In the United States, as in no other country, institutions of higher learning are directed fundamentally by the men and women who serve as members of boards of higher education. These boards have no common title. They are designated variously as boards of trustees, regents, governors, visitors, overseers, and the like. Their range of responsibilities varies from limited to complete control of a system of higher institutions, but is more commonly limited to responsibility governing one college or university.

The recognition given by the American people to the public service rendered by persons who serve on college and university boards of trustees is strong and of long standing. Beyond this prestige and appreciation, however, relatively little has been done to help trustees gain better insights into the character of the duties that they are expected to perform. Until recent years, neither society at large nor the professional community provided much orientation or tangible assistance to college trustees. A trustee most often got an overview of his authority and responsibility only from the charter and bylaws of the institution.

Inclusion of this monograph in the Library of Education series is, therefore, a significant part of a new trend. It is a long step forward in reducing the paucity of usable information available to college and university boards of trustees. First, it identifies and describes the different types of boards responsible for higher education now operating in the country; second, it notes and discusses a wide span of important issues and problems that surround these boards in their work; finally, it points out the gaps in knowledge about boards of higher education and the areas in which more research and scholarly effort are needed.

Consistent with the procedures followed in the series, this book is based essentially on a thorough review of the information available at the time of its writing. It draws on a wide range of resources, both published and unpublished, and of both current and historical interest. It goes on, however, to interpret and evaluate the aggregate of authoritative opinions, research findings, and scholarly thought about trustees and their roles in college and university administration. In so doing it gives a clearer meaning to current and emerging conditions under which higher institutions operate. Attention is consistently focused on the ways in which the effectiveness of boards of trustees can be extended to meet modern problems. Suggestions for doing this are advanced both for the trustees themselves and for the professional specialists who work with them.

The contents of this monograph will be most useful to members of the boards of higher education. It will be useful also for presidents of colleges and universities and persons on their administrative staffs. Students of the practice and theory of administration of higher education will find it a valuable reference in guiding their teaching and research efforts. Governors, legislators, and all others who give direction to colleges and universities in the United States will find the monograph rewarding reading.

ERNEST V. HOLLIS
*Director, College and University
Administration Branch
Division of Higher Education
U.S. Office of Education*

Contents

College Boards of Trustees

CHAPTER I

A Background for Understanding
College Boards of Trustees

Most colleges and universities in the United States are controlled by a board which has been given official legal authority to govern all aspects of the institution. These boards are usually made up of lay citizens rather than professional educators and are designated by a wide range of titles. The most common of these is "Board of Trustees."

Whether the boards are designated as the "Board of Trustees," "Board of Regents," "Board of Visitors," "Board of Directors," or "Members of the Corporation," the salient fact about these boards is that they are the responsible controlling agency of the institutions. Very often, therefore, the board is referred to as the "governing board" or "board of control" of the college or university. By virtue of constitutional or statutory designation in the case of publicly sponsored institutions, and through charter or articles of incorporation in the case of privately sponsored ones, the board of trustees is constituted a body corporate. By this is meant that, with regard to the legal basis of operations of the institution for which it is named, the board is responsible and empowered as a single body; no one or several members of the board can assume the obligations or rights of the total group. Legally the board is viewed as one individual: it can hold property, sue and be sued, enter into contractual agreements, and generally exercise—on behalf of the institution—the privileges accorded an individual citizen with respect to personal property rights and business operations.

An understanding of the nature and development of this fundamental legal concept of the board of trustees as a corporate body in its relationships to and on behalf of the institution controlled is a first step in acquiring a clear concept of the government of higher education in America. The concept has been repeatedly asserted in the laws relating to college and university operations and in court cases interpreting these laws. In this monograph and in many other works on this subject, reference is often made to the idea of the corporate status of boards of trustees. Yet the fact remains that much of the misunderstandings and problems which arise in institutional operations and inter-agency relations involving colleges and universities stem from the fact that this basic concept is often overlooked or not accepted.

Because board members are part of a corporate body and therefore have no legal authority to act as individuals for the institution, the title "trustee" is not strictly correct. This inaccuracy was noted some thirty years ago when Russell and Reeves called attention to the fact that the term "trustee" is a misnomer because the board of trustees of a college does not normally exercise the same responsibilities that are attached to a trusteeship in commercial parlance.[1] Yet the use of the term persists. Three decades ago a study covering 640 American institutions operating at that time found that 76.5 per cent of them had controlling bodies designated as "boards of trustees." [2]

More recently an analysis of the boards of over a thousand higher institutions showed that of thirty-five different names used, boards of control are designated as "boards of trustees," for almost two-thirds of all institutions and for more than 80 per cent of the privately controlled institutions.[3]

An understanding of the concept of the board as a corporate body is therefore necessary to a sound appreciation of the control of institutions of higher learning in America. Also necessary is the knowledge that an institution's operations are often influenced and directed by boards other than the board of control. Such boards with legal powers over higher institutions, colleges and universities, are designated as "coordinating boards" or "governing and coordinating boards" in this monograph and are discussed along with governing or controlling boards.

---

[1] John Dale Russell and Floyd W. Reeves, *The Evaluation of Higher Institutions* (Chicago: The University of Chicago Press, 1936), p. 18.

[2] Alfred Williams Anthony, "Concerning College Trustees," *Bulletin of the Association of American Colleges,* XIX (December, 1933), 425-31.

[3] Walter Crosby Eells, "Boards of Control of Universities and Colleges," The Educational Record, XLII (October, 1961), 336.

The Board of Control—The American Idea

There are now operating in the United States almost 2000 boards responsible for higher education. A study by the author and Hollis found 519 boards responsible for publicly controlled institutions in 1958–59. Of the total, 209 were boards which in membership was representative of the entire state and responsibility often extended to more than one college or university; 310 were local institutional boards and almost all of these were named for the control of public two-year colleges.[4] No comparable study is yet available covering privately controlled higher education. Since the general practice in the governance of privately sponsored institutions is for each one to be independent of others, however, it may be presumed that there are nearly as many boards as there are privately controlled institutions. Thus the total number probably approaches 2000.

In no other nation has the power of direction and control of the vital function of higher education been decentralized and delegated in this fashion. The practice in the United States is strikingly different from that in other nations not only in the high decentralization of authority for higher education, but in the fact that the holders of that authority are laymen. The large majority of individual members of these boards are not professionally engaged in the business of higher education. In these facts lies the source of much of the strength of American higher education, and, paradoxically, many of its weaknesses.

The use of boards to direct colleges and universities did not come about in this country by deliberate plan or action. Indeed, the original idea came from other lands. But in the United States the idea has flourished to highest use both in terms of numbers of persons, institutions, and students involved, and in dedication to the idea as a principle in administering colleges and universities. To understand the evolution of the principle it is necessary to look back to the origins of higher education in the nation and to the changes that have taken place in the last century.

---

[4] S. V. Martorana and Ernest V. Hollis, *State Boards Responsible for Higher Education,* U.S. Office of Education Circular OE-53005 (Washington, D.C.: USGPO, 1960), pp. 183-98.

The Influence of Patterns of
Higher Education in Other Nations

America, the melting pot of peoples during the eighteenth, nine-teenth, and early twentieth centuries, was also a melting pot of ideas. Immigrants coming in successive waves to the new country naturally carried with them notions of higher education—both its function and its structure—from the lands from which they came. For a time the earlier institutions reflected sharply the influence of prototypes in European nations. Gradually, however, the elements of similarity were varied to fit a new society and a new culture. And new types of institutions of higher learning quite unique to the United States emerged.

At the time that the American colonists first began to become concerned with the founding of institutions of learning beyond the common school level, Oxford and Cambridge were the predominant centers of higher learning in England. These institutions, therefore, became the models of university structure which the early American institutions were designed to implement.

Organizationally speaking, however, the English universities were not tightly knit administrative structures. They were rather com-posites of colleges, each with its own clearly defined student body and faculty operating largely autonomously one from the other.

Modern scholars of the history of higher education are carrying on an interesting debate in their writings concerning which early European universities have been most influential in molding the character of those operating in the United States. There seems to be little disagreement on the point, however, that much of the pres-ent structure of American institutions even at the board of control level can be traced back to earlier European practices.

Some scholars attach greater weight to the influence of English universities, others to that of eighteenth century Scottish institutions. Brubacher and Rudy, in their discussion of the subject, state:

> Although even Harvard was not immune to Scottish influence, it was at William and Mary that it was felt most directly. The charter Blair obtained for the Virginia school resembled that of a Scottish "unicollege" institution. Like Aberdeen, Glasgow, King's and Marischal, it incorporated both a university and a degree-granting college by a single letter-patent. At the same time, a governing

board was created made up of members of the nonacademic community; this was, in characteristic Scottish fashion, to have real administrative authority over the college.[5]

The historical influence of European universities on American higher education has been traced by some scholars to early medieval universities, the first centers of higher learning in Western culture. Professor Cowley, in a report of one such effort, has concluded that:

> European universities have followed two historical patterns of government, the French and the Italian. American colleges see-sawed between the two until the beginning of the nineteenth century and then chose the Italian. . . . I call it the historic Italian plan, but the Americans got it from the Scottish universities which had copied it from the University of Leyden, which in turn had adopted it from the Italian universities.[6]

The chief difference between the French universities and the Italian was in the administrative control of the institution. The former placed the government of the institutions in the hands of the faculty. In medieval Italian universities, on the other hand, the students were the group in power: they held all administrative posts and made both administrative and legislative decisions. When this control was lost by the students in an evolutionary process encompassing many decades, Cowley points out ". . . civil authorities took over by appointing what we would today call boards of trustees, that is, lay bodies of non-academic people. They became the governors of both professors and students."[7]

Once having been recognized in the organization for government of the first institutions in what is now the United States—Harvard, Yale, William and Mary, Princeton, and others in the Eastern states—the principle of placing primary responsibility for the direction of colleges and universities in the hands of boards of lay citizens has never been challenged. Instead it has grown steadily in strength and public acceptance. This may be attributed perhaps not only to the advantages that have been observed to accrue to both the institutions and their constituencies through the principle of administration

---

[5] John S. Brubacher and Willis Rudy, *Higher Education in Transition: An American History: 1636-1956* (New York: Harper & Row, Publishers, 1958), p. 5.

[6] W. H. Cowley, "The Administration of American Colleges and Universities," in *University Administration Practice*, Oswald Nielsen, ed. (Stanford, Calif.: Stanford University, Graduate School of Business, 1959), pp. 7-8.

[7] *Ibid.*, p. 8.

by lay boards, but also to the fact that the advantages of the same principle have been observed throughout the history of the nation in the government of public elementary and secondary schools.

Historical Adaptability of American Institutions of Higher Learning

As social, economic, and cultural conditions in the United States changed, higher education had also to change to fulfill its functions. Adaptability has historically characterized post-high school education in this country. Consequent modifications in the government of higher institutions and the role of boards of trustees also occurred.

The adaptability of American higher education is shown by changes in individual institutions. The older institutions of higher learning in the United States are today very different from what they were a hundred years ago. The colleges then had considerably more unity of purpose, homogeneity of students and faculty, and simplicity of administrative structure. "The unity of the early nineteenth century liberal college," claim Ruml and Morrison, "began to break down with the industrialization and urbanization of American society." Of the many influences that probably contributed to this change they assert that three were decisive: "the specialization of knowledge and its pursuit, the introduction of the elective system, and changes in the motivation for 'going to college.' " [8]

Another way that the higher learning in America has shown its adaptability is in the emergence of entirely new types of institutions. The development of new types of educational units to carry out special services for the people and the economy seems to be a social phenomenon especially characteristic of the United States. The pattern that it has taken has also tended to influence the place and function of boards of trustees in the administration of modern colleges and universities.

The era of autonomy and start of a tradition. Most of the early American colleges were established and authorized to operate as separate and independent institutions. This was true of both privately and publicly controlled colleges. Each had its own board of trustees to which the state granted—through charter, constitution,

---

[8] Beardsley Ruml and Donald H. Morrison, *Memo To A College Trustee: A Report of the Financial and Structural Problems of the Liberal College* (New York: McGraw-Hill Book Company, 1959), p. 47.

or statute—wide autonomous powers. This procedure was consistent with the times and the primary purpose of the institution.

Early American institutions, particularly those sponsored by private agencies, appear to have been founded primarily for the purpose of meeting theological needs for trained personnel. Their governing boards were in general termed "boards of trustees" and were composed mainly of clergymen who exercised executive and administrative as well as governing authority in the institution.

In time the American middle class began to emerge and traditional humanistic studies and college programs began to assume a new aspect. Industrialization brought a growing demand for college programs to prepare new kinds of professional and technical manpower. As a result, the second half of the nineteenth century saw a gradual change in the character of the older colleges, ultimately resulting in the "elective" system of programming students' studies and the awarding of a variety of degrees.

As early as 1850, Francis Wayland, president of Brown University, wrote the challenging "Report to the Corporation of Brown University on Changes in the System of Collegiate Instruction." The report called attention to the fact that the American college was not furnishing the type of education suited to the times and to the "needs of the community." He placed responsibility for correcting the situation on trustees who had "visitorial" power to appraise and direct the University. Although the suggestions for curriculum changes for training professional and skilled men were not immediately adopted by Brown University, they began to be incorporated in the programs of Cornell University and other private colleges and in the state universities that were springing up across the nation.[9] These changes heightened popular interest in higher education and led to new responsibilities for boards of trustees.

Still operating autonomously, some of the colleges grew in scope and complexity into true universities. Among the older colleges Harvard University led the way by incorporating new graduate programs and Johns Hopkins and Clark Universities, starting as modern German university type graduate schools, soon began to

---

9 "Francis Wayland's Thoughts on the Present Collegiate System, 1842," in *American Higher Education: A Documentary History,* Richard Hofstadter and Wilson Smith, eds. (Chicago: The University of Chicago Press, 1961), Vol. I, pp. 334-49.

challenge the supremacy of European universities in research and graduate studies.

Land-grant colleges and state universities.   The development of large and renowned universities was not confined to private auspices. By 1857, fifteen states had received land grants for the endowment of state universities. The Universities of Michigan, Minnesota, and Virginia, for example, were already well known and becoming stronger. Some of the early state universities were partially under private control but gradually became completely state-controlled.

By the Land Grant Act of 1862, Congress encouraged the creation of a new type of public higher institution—the land-grant college—which was aimed at furnishing instruction in agriculture and the mechanical arts. Some states, such as New York, established the new college as part of an existing private university; others, such as Minnesota, established it as part of an existing state university; and still others founded it as a separate institution. In *Colleges for Our Land and Time*, Edward D. Eddy describes the effect of this movement on governing boards:

> In almost all states the institutions were separated from the existing government organization. A separate board of trustees was created, responsible to the state administration and legislature. This was a significant action in the early days. Historically, by and large, it has prevented political control and influence and has kept state-supported higher education sufficiently isolated from the machinations of changing political regimes.[10]

The latter observation is questionable, especially in the light of recent studies of the control of these institutions (see Chapter V). At any rate, their control added a new dimension to federal-state relationship in higher education, and a new concept of state-board relations.

It is significant that the land-grant colleges were conceived and established as autonomous units, more closely akin to chartered independent private colleges than to a coherent or integrated state system of higher education. A new type of control was foreshadowed, however, by the new boards, which were composed of

---

[10] Edward Danforth Eddy, Jr., *Colleges for Our Land and Time* (New York: Harper & Row, Publishers, 1956), p. 51.

farmers, businessmen, engineers, and lawyers—as well as ministers, who had been predominant on early private college boards.

Although it was not planned that the land-grant college or the land-grant college and state university combined should develop into a statewide system of higher education, this has in fact occurred in many states. The University of Wisconsin and Pennsylvania State University, for example, have developed multiple campus networks which blanket their entire respective states.

Expansion of land-grant colleges and state universities into statewide systems of higher education has also brought about changes in the role and function of the boards of trustees. The governing board of such a system becomes not just the controlling agency of a single institution but the controlling and coordinating agency for several institutional units. The duties and outlook of a governing and coordinating board (see Chapter II) are quite different from the controlling board of a single institution in a number of important aspects. Directly and indirectly, boards of trustees of privately controlled colleges and publicly controlled institutions are influenced by the evolution of statewide systems of higher institutions under governing and coordinating boards.

Normal schools, teachers colleges and state colleges.   The emergence and growth of state normal schools, later to become in most instances teachers colleges, state colleges, and in some cases state universities, is another thread in the fabric of American higher education and the development of present-day boards of higher education. Though now clearly recognized institutions of higher learning, the teachers colleges originated in response to needs quite different from those which gave rise to the state universities and land-grant colleges.

The growth of public elementary and secondary schools in the latter part of the nineteenth century intensified the demand for teachers, to whose training little attention had been given. The first state-supported normal school established solely for teacher preparation opened at Lexington, Massachusetts, in 1839. By 1860, the teacher training course, which originally lasted eleven weeks, had extended to two years.[11] Other states followed Massachusetts and by 1889

---

[11] Charles A. Harper, *A Century of Public Teacher Education* (Washington, D.C.: Hugh Birch-Horace Mann Fund, National Education Association, 1939), p. 35.

there were 23 State Boards of Education among the 38 states and a system of teacher certification by examination; by 1890 there were 92 state-supported normal schools.[12] From their beginnings these schools were governed by boards which were representative of the state as a whole and were coordinated on a statewide basis.

As more people aspired to high school education, the normal schools expanded their curriculum and became teachers colleges, joining private liberal arts colleges and state universities in offering programs to prepare high school teachers. Around 1920 a four-year course became standard. During the last twenty years, the function of these institutions has become more truly that of a liberal arts college dedicated to teacher preparation. With the greater freedom for development suggested and permitted under the simple designation "state colleges," these institutions have in many cases added programs for training workers in other specialized fields, particularly business and engineering.

Because of their history, the teachers colleges and state colleges in most states are under the jurisdiction of the State Board of Education, or a separate state-level board for state colleges (as in Minnesota). Generally a higher degree of coordination in all phases is to be found among these institutions than in other types of higher institutions. Here again, then, it is seen that the board of trustees is either a governing and coordinating board of a statewide system of institutions or simply a coordinating board if the institutions have, in addition to the state-level board, their own immediate governing boards (as in the case of Kentucky).

Municipal four-year institutions.   Colleges and universities that operate under the public auspices of particular municipalities have also shown changes in character over the years. Some of these institutions had their origins in private schools, while others began their operations under the control and financing of municipal or local school governments. In 1939, the U.S. Office of Education directory of higher institutions listed 23 municipal four-year colleges and universities; in the 1959 edition only 16 were identified; but in 1961 the number had risen to 23.[13]

---

[12] Richard Hofstadter and C. DeWitt Hardy, *The Development and Scope of Higher Education in the U.S.* (New York: Columbia University Press, 1952), p. 95.

[13] *Directory of Education,* Part 3: *Higher Education,* 1939-40; 1959-60; 1961-62, U.S. Office of Education (Washington, D.C.: USGPO, 1940, 1960, 1962).

There is evidence in the history of some institutions—for example, Wayne State University—that as public municipal four-year colleges grow and assume a broader scope of service, they tend to be made a part of the total state system of higher education. The change appears to be caused by the necessity for a broader base of financing, control, and coordination. When this transition from municipal to state control occurs, the institution usually is either made responsible to a new board of trustees of statewide representation or is placed under an existing board responsible for the control of one or more other state higher institutions.

Two-year colleges. A relative newcomer to the family of higher institutions in America, being only some fifty years old, is the two-year college, perhaps most appropriately called the "community college." It is found listed also under various terms such as "junior college" and "technical institute." The establishment of these schools has increased rapidly in recent years under the stimuli of growing demands for higher education, increasing state support for such of these institutions as are publicly sponsored, and growing recognition by private agencies—such as the Roman Catholic Church—which are committed to maintenance of a relatively complete educational system to serve particular constituencies. Now there are over 600 institutions of the two-year type listed in the U. S. Office of Education directory of institutions. Together they enroll approximately a seventh of all students attending college and enrolled in programs leading to a bachelor's degree. Both the number of institutions of this type and their enrollments are growing rapidly.[14]

Privately controlled two-year colleges are governed by boards of trustees that are quite similar in character to those that govern privately controlled four-year colleges and universities. The control of public institutions of this type varies from complete local control by a governing board which is also the board of trustees of the local public elementary and secondary schools, through local or regional boards of trustees responsible only for the two-year colleges, to complete state control by a board which has membership representative of the entire state. Often two-year campuses are found as part of statewide systems of higher education under single board control.[15]

14 Edith Huddleston, "Opening College Enrollment, Fall, 1961," *Higher Education,* XVIII (January-February, 1962), 12-16.

15 S. V. Martorana and D. G. Morrison, *Patterns of Organization and Support of Public Two-Year Colleges,* U.S. Office of Education Circular OE-52000 (Washington, D.C.: USGPO, 1957).

Privately controlled 4-year colleges and universities. The fore-going discussion has centered heavily on the emergence of new types of publicly controlled higher institutions as indication of the adaptability of higher education in America. It should not be concluded from this, however, that privately controlled four-year colleges and universities are lagging behind in readiness to change administrative structure and programs to meet new conditions. On the contrary, much of the experimentation and innovation in higher education during the last fifty to one hundred years was first developed in privately controlled institutions.

Recognition of the need to change, not only with respect to the character and organization of individual institutions, but also in departing in some measure from the traditional practice of autonomous institutional operation, is quite evident among the privately controlled higher institutions today. Illustrations of this alertness and readiness to change to meet modern demands are seen in the formation of the Claremont Graduate School by joint action of three independent Southern California colleges, in the contractual relations for the Joint Center for Urban Studies negotiated by Harvard and Massachusetts Institute of Technology, and in the Joint University Libraries in Nashville, Tennessee in which George Peabody College for Teachers, Scarritt College for Christian Workers, and Vanderbilt University are cooperating.[16]

Implications for Boards of Trustees

Out of the evolution of the higher education in America has come a complex of colleges and universities different from that found in any other nation. The observation is made frequently that in this country there is not a "system of higher education" but many systems and subsystems of higher institutions. In part this is because in the United States responsibility for education constitutionally resides with the individual states. Perhaps in even larger measure it has come about because leadership and the highest level of administrative responsibility for American colleges and universities was vested from the start in lay persons representative of and close to the institutions' constituencies.

---

[16] S. V. Martorana and James C. Messersmith, *Cooperative Projects Among Colleges and Universities,* U.S. Office of Education Circular No. 649 (Washington, D.C.: USGPO, 1961), pp. 8-16.

Patterns of administrative organization of higher institutions are continuing to change. Russell described the nature and extent of these changes and attributed them largely to changes in the size of institutions.[17] Change in size has in turn been a function of adaptation to other social and economic changes in the nation. Cowley asserts that: "To comprehend the structuring of American higher education four concepts must be understood: first, diversity; second, equalitarianism; third, local control; and fourth, our mixed state and private enterprise." [18]

It is imperative to the continued sound growth and development of American higher education that boards of trustees, college staff members, and the public at large understand the role of trustees in governing colleges and universities. As stewards acting for larger interests in the society, the trustees themselves must maintain an awareness and understanding of the changing character, not only of the institution or institutions which they direct, but also of higher education as a totality. The charge addressed to the trustees of the liberal college by Ruml and Morrison may well be directed in this country to members of boards of control of all types of institutions:

> The colleges are part of the shadow government of the United States; they have status, duties, and freedom. . . . The Trustees of the liberal colleges are participating in an historic period on a strategic front. Let them be informed so that they can discharge their responsibilities with courage and with wisdom.[19]

---

[17] John Dale Russell, "Changing Patterns of Administration in Higher Education," *Annals of the American Academy of Political and Social Science, CCCI* (September, 1955), 22-31.

[18] W. H. Cowley, *op. cit.,* p. 5.

[19] Beardsley Ruml and Donald H. Morrison, *op. cit.,* p. 94.

CHAPTER II

Types of Boards of Trustees

Boards of trustees which have the legal and official duty of directing colleges and universities do not number in a one to one ratio to the institutions. This is because in some instances a single institution is directed by more than one board, even though one may be officially designated the governing board of the college; in other cases two or more institutions are directed by a common board. An illustration of the first situation is the New Mexico Board of Educational Finance, which controls budgetary matters for the state-supported colleges and universities in New Mexico. An example of a board which controls a system of colleges is the State College Board in Minnesota.

Whenever more than one board has an official authority over the affairs of colleges and universities, the boards involved have different spheres of responsibility and separate functions to perform. It is possible, therefore, to categorize boards in terms of the functions which they are officially intended to fulfill. A second basis of classification examines and classifies boards in terms of the legal source from which they receive authority to operate.

Classifications Based on Functions

Recent studies of boards responsible for higher education have brought forth a variety of terms to depict classification according to function. Glenny divided official statewide agencies with authority over higher institutions into "governing" and "coordinating" agencies, defining the first type as one which in effect supplants all individual institutional boards of control, and the second type as one superimposed over existing boards.[1] Martorana and Hollis identified 209 boards responsible for higher education and classified them as follows:

---

[1] Lyman A. Glenny, *Autonomy of Public Colleges: The Challenge of Coordination* (New York: McGraw-Hill Book Company, 1959), p. 34.

Governing board: A board which is legally charged with the direct control and operation of only a single institutional unit.

Coordinating board: A board which is legally responsible for organizing, regulating, or otherwise bringing together the overall policies or functions (or both) in areas such as planning, budgeting, and programing, but which does not have authority to govern institutions.

Governing-coordinating board: A board having legal responsibility for functioning both as a coordinating board and a governing board for two or more institutional units which offer programs that have common elements.

Other board: A board having responsibility at the State level for supervising, accrediting, certifying, advising, or performing a similar function in relation to public higher education institutions, but which does not have specific authority to govern these institutions or to coordinate their operations.[2]

That a classification of boards based on their function could be devised which would be accepted as standard throughout the United States is doubtful. Differences in tradition, legal status, and practice from state to state preclude a precise definition and classification of boards which manage higher institutions.

The governing board. As reported earlier in this monograph, the governing board or institutional board of control is the oldest type of board responsible for higher education in the United States. In the early days of higher education this was the only type of board and there was therefore, a one to one numerical relationship between boards and institutions. Although the language and the type of authorization varied, the conclusion was clear that the board was to be responsible in all respects for the operation of the institution.

The practice of having a single board of trustees to oversee and manage all the affairs of a single institution of higher learning is still predominant in the nation. Among the colleges and universities that are privately controlled this is almost the only type of board to be found. A few, such as the boards of trustees of St. Louis University and Brigham Young University, could be classified as governing *and* coordinating boards because there are several subsidiary institutions affiliated under the general jurisdiction of the board. The practice of establishing branch institutions is relatively undeveloped

---

[2] S. V. Martorana and Ernest V. Hollis, *State Boards Responsible for Higher Education,* U.S. Office of Education Circular OE-53005 (Washington, D.C.: USGPO, 1960), p. 6.

as yet among privately controlled colleges and universities, so that coordination as a particular problem or function of the board of trustees is not significant.

Even among the publicly supported and controlled institutions of higher education, the governing boards are still most common. As seen in Table 1, in 1959 approximately four out of five boards with responsibility for publicly controlled colleges in the fifty states were classified as governing boards.

Closer examination of the data on which Table 1 is based, however, raises some doubts about the future of the practice of administering public colleges which offer programs of four or more years by maintaining only institutional governing boards. The first observation is that the governing boards listed in the table overwhelmingly represent public two-year colleges, which as a general rule have a strong local orientation and are supported by both local and state funds. Many also are the result of an upward extension of the local elementary and secondary schools. Because of these antecedents, and their philosophical identification with local educational services, these two-year colleges will very probably continue to have local institutional boards of control.

A second observation casting doubt on the permanence of the predominance of governing boards as sole agencies for directing public four-year institutions is the present number of boards, and the trend toward developing more boards which have governing responsibility for more than one institution. These governing and coordinating boards are quite common even in the northeastern and north-central regions of the country, where the traditions of autonomous, independently operating institutions are most influential.

The governing and coordinating board.   Several factors have caused the sizable number of boards which have responsibility for coordinating several colleges and universities as well as governing or managing them. One historical factor was the placing of the normal schools under the state boards of education. Twenty-two of the governing-coordinating boards shown in Table 1 had their origin in the normal school movement in their respective states.

A number of states have made a single board responsible for governing and coordinating all public higher education in the state. Four states have such boards: Georgia, North Dakota, Rhode Island, and South Dakota. Hawaii and Nevada also have only one

TABLE 1
Distribution of 209 State Boards Responsible for Public Higher Education, by Type, Region, and State, 1959

Region and State	Total number of boards	Governing boards	Governing coordinating boards	Coordinating boards	Other boards
1	2	3	4	5	6
NORTHEAST	39	22	12		5
Connecticut	2		2		
Maine	3	1	2		
Massachusetts	8	5	1		2
New Hampshire ...	2	1	1		
New Jersey	2		2		
New York	2		1		1
Pennsylvania	17	14	1		2
Rhode Island	1		1		
Vermont	2	1	1		
NORTH-CENTRAL	46	20	15	1	10
Illinois	5	1	2		2
Indiana	4		3		1
Iowa	2		1		1
Kansas	2		1		1
Michigan	6	5	1		
Minnesota	3		2		
Missouri	8	7			1
Nebraska	4	1	1		2
North Dakota	1		1		
Ohio	6	6			
South Dakota	1		1		
Wisconsin	4		2	1	1
SOUTH	86	49	24	5	8
Alabama	4	3	1		
Arkansas	8	7	1		
Delaware	3	2			1
Florida	2		1		1
Georgia	1		1		
Kentucky	8	6		1	1
Louisiana	2		2		
Maryland	5	2	2		1
Mississippi	4		1		3
North Carolina ...	14	11	2	1	
Oklahoma	7	4	2	1	
South Carolina	6	6			
Tennessee	2		2		
Texas	11	6	3	1	1
Virginia	7	2	4	1	
West Virginia	2		2		
MOUNTAIN	24	9	10	2	3
Arizona	2		1		1
Colorado	5	1	3		1
Idaho	1		1		
Montana	1		1		
Nevada	1		1		
New Mexico	8	7		1	
Utah	4		3	1	
Wyoming	2	1			1
PACIFIC	14	8	4		2
Alaska	2		1		1
California	3	1	2		
Oregon	2	1	1		
Washington	6	5			1
Hawaii	1	1			
Total	209	108	65	8	28

Adapted from S. V. Martorana and Ernest V. Hollis, *State Boards Responsible for Higher Education*, p. 16.

board responsible for all public higher education. In these two cases, however, the state university is the only institution for which each board is responsible.

Arizona, Florida, Idaho, Iowa, Kansas, Mississippi, Montana, and Oregon cannot be classified as having a single board responsible for governing and coordinating all public higher education in the state, because in these cases the two-year colleges are under separate institutional governing boards. In these states, however, all other publicly supported institutions are governed and coordinated by a single board representative of the state.

A more recent factor tending to place greater emphasis on co-ordination is the founding of branch institutions by well-established state universities and land-grant colleges. Twenty-seven of the 65 governing-coordinating boards reported in Table 1 are representative of state universities and land-grant colleges.

Illustrations of the impact on the duties and burden of responsibility borne by a board of a state university or land-grant college that undertakes to perform a statewide function by creating a network of institutions are seen in the experiences of Pennsylvania State University, the University of Wisconsin, and the two major institutions in Indiana, Purdue and Indiana Universities. Before World War II all these state universities except Indiana were operating essentially single-campus institutions. Their boards were aware of a responsibility to provide higher educational services on a statewide basis as evidenced by the well-developed programs of general extension. These services, however, consisted essentially of individual courses and were carried on in facilities which were either rented or loaned by local public school authorities.

The influx of veterans after the war and the passage of the first G. I. Bill put these state universities and others under considerable pressure to admit students in numbers beyond the capacity of the main campuses. The result was a heightening and formalizing of general extension programs in some places into full-scale centers for resident instruction. Usually this happened in centers of population too far from the main campus for daily commuting by students.

From these beginnings there developed statewide systems of higher education which in 1961-62 in Indiana included Purdue University, with four branches and a total enrollment in excess of 20,000 students, and Indiana University, with two campuses and nine centers and over 28,000 students; in Wisconsin, the University of Wisconsin with two campuses and over eight centers with a total enrollment of more than 32,000 students; and in Pennsylvania, the Pennsylvania State University with thirteen Commonwealth campuses serving in all more than 21,000 students.

There is a difference both in degree and in kind in the problems of government faced by the board of trustees responsible for such a statewide system as compared to the tasks faced by the board of trustees of even a very large university operating only at one location. In the former case the board is faced with the job of planning for and channelling the growth and overseeing the operation of what amounts to several institutions, a task quite different from governing only one.

An illustration of the special complications that a governing-coordinating board is apt to encounter is seen in both Wisconsin and Pennsylvania. In these states the legislatures have established arrangements whereby local areas served by a branch of the state university can finance facilities to house programs of instruction at that branch. Quite likely these arrangements would involve the board of trustees at times when policy concerning the use of the facilities is to be set, if not before.

Another recent development is the increase in the number of boards classifiable as governing-coordinating. This is the tendency of boards of trustees in large cities to create multiple unit systems. For instance, there are now in existence four four-year and three three-year colleges in the newly created New York City University, and seven campuses of the Los Angeles Junior College District.

Number of institutions responsible to governing-coordinating boards. A question frequently raised concerning this type of board is: How many institutions can a board both govern and coordinate effectively? A definitive answer to this question would have to take into account the size of the institutions and their geographic dispersal, the character of the programs, and related factors. Some general insight, however, into the problem of the manageable span of control by boards over institutions can perhaps be gained from an examination of the number of institutional units for which governing-coordinating boards are responsible.

In 1959 there were 359 institutional units—that is, clearly recognizable colleges or universities or branches of such colleges encompassing at least two years of instruction, responsible to the 65 governing-coordinating state boards shown in Table 1. The range of number of units headed by a given board was from two to 28 and the average was between five and six.

Although all governing-coordinating boards carry the dual responsibility of governing and coordinating a multi-institutional system, there are those—usually State Boards of Education—which in addition to this responsibility have a general state-level supervisory duty for other colleges governed by local boards. This fact and the diversity of types of institutions directed by governing-coordinating boards make it difficult to determine the limits of board capability in this function. The Regents of the State of Georgia, for example, are at the head of a much more complex system than the Board of Education of State Normal Schools in Nebraska. In the absence of penetrating study and the development of equitable, objective criteria for measurement of performance, it is impossible to assess the limits of successful accomplishment of the governing-coordinating function of either of the more complex or the more simple system. To date such criteria have not been developed.

There is some feeling among those involved in higher education administration that the limits of human energy and attention prohibit too large a span of institutional control for a given board of trustees. Not only is there concern lest the trustees have a physically unmanageable task to perform, but there is also fear that too widely divergent types of institutions might be made the responsibility of the same board. Sometimes it may seem very logical for this to be done, but doing so may deprive some of the institutions involved of what Selznick calls "institutional integrity." He says: "The fallacy of combining agencies on the basis of logical association of functions is a characteristic result of the failure to take account of institutional integrity." [3] Preservation of a desirable measure of institutional autonomy while simultaneously guaranteeing the strength of the total system of colleges is the final test of successful coordination. To this end Martorana and Hollis concluded:

> Depending on the size and complexity of the units, such a board [sic., governing-coordinating] should be responsible for not more than 6–9 institutions. With a larger number, a condition develops

[3] Philip Selznick, *Leadership in Administration* (New York: Harper & Row, Publishers, 1957), p. 58.

which may be termed "presidential control," as opposed to "board control" of the institutions in the system. This encourages too great an assumption of authority in the administrative head of each unit and weakens the vital principle of lay board control to which this country is fully committed.[4]

The coordinating board. The most recent type of board responsible for higher education is that which has no responsibility for controlling or governing any institution but has instead a duty to coordinate a number of institutions and to guide the overall development of higher education in a state. Such strictly coordinating boards are found in the States of Arkansas, Illinois, Kentucky, New Mexico, North Carolina, Oklahoma, Texas, Utah, Virginia, and Wisconsin. The Coordinating Council in California also is of this type. Eight of these boards have come into being since 1950; the most recent is the one in Arkansas which was established by the 1961 legislature. The one in Illinois was reconstituted in 1961 with somewhat more powers than were held by its predecessor. Only the Oklahoma State Regents for Higher Education antedates the year 1950, having been established in 1941.

Apparently, a coordinating board can be so conceived, structured, and staffed as to enable it to coordinate effectively as many institutions as exist in a state. This is evident in the fact that a number of the existing statewide coordinating boards are responsible for coordinating all publicly supported and controlled higher education including public two-year colleges. This is true in the cases of all of the ten states cited above with the exception of Illinois and Texas, where the public two-year colleges are under the state-level jurisdiction, respectively, of the State Department of Education and the Texas Education Agency. Note that in New Mexico, Utah, Virginia, and Wisconsin the coordination of education of the junior-college type is through the boards of trustees of the major state universities which operate extensive systems of two-year branches in each of these states.

Boards with other functions. It is doubtful if there is anywhere available now a compilation which describes completely or provides even a complete listing of all boards which have some measure of responsibility for higher education. Responsibilities within state official channels for "accrediting," "regulating," "supervising," "certify-

---

[4] Martorana and Hollis, *op. cit.,* p. 19.

ing," and "licensing," are frequently placed in special boards or commissions. In most instances such functions as listed above are made the responsibility of the State Board of Education, but this is not always true. There is, for example, a State Teacher Certification Board in Illinois, a Board of Collegiate Authority which approves degrees in Massachusetts, and a Community College Commission in Mississippi and Wyoming.

The existence of these "other" boards which have jurisdiction of one type or another over colleges and universities shows again that it is fallacious to think of boards of higher education in the United States as being of a particular type. There are, in fact, several types of boards responsible for colleges and universities, and to understand higher education in the nation an awareness and appreciation of the variety of boards is necessary.

Classification of Boards
According to Legal Basis for Authority

Colleges and universities, just like any business or commercial enterprise, must have a legal basis for operating. Practices in the several states whereby official status is given to colleges and universities vary greatly. Some states provide extensive requirements which are closely controlled; other states provide virtually no regulation at all.

In the final analysis, the state constitutions and the statutes enacted by state legislatures are the source of authority for a board of trustees to operate a college or university, whether it is publicly or privately controlled. The procedure in any particular state is outlined in the state constitution and in the compiled statutes or legal code governing higher education and procedures for incorporation. Each of the fifty states has provided legal foundation for both publicly and privately controlled institutions of higher learning.

Contrary to many other nations, the United States has no federal system of centralized regulation of higher education. The Constitution is silent on the matter of control of education, so the Tenth Amendment reserves this responsibility for the states. With a few notable exceptions, the boards of control of all higher educational institutions in the United States receive their authority from one of the states. The exceptions are the military service academies at West

Point, Annapolis, and Colorado Springs, the several maritime academies, the Graduate School of the U.S. Department of Agriculture, and the junior college of the Panama Canal Zone, which is also under federal auspices. The universities that are located in the District of Columbia also are chartered by the federal government.

An examination of the laws in the several states shows that boards of trustees and institutions are given a legal basis through one of two methods. One of these is by direct approval through the state constitution or specific statutory enactment. Another is through approval by an official agency which itself is established by the state constitution or by statute and is given the responsibility of approving higher institutions. This may be an agency such as a state board of education or a state council of higher education, with jurisdiction only over educational institutions, or it may be an agency responsible for the state's system of incorporation of all enterprises—educational, business, philanthropic, or other. A study by J. H. McNeely which examined colleges and universities as parts of the government of the states in which they were located found three different types of boards of state supported higher institutions. He defined these as (1) constitutional boards—those having their origins in the state constitution, (2) incorporated boards—those having been created as corporate bodies and given certain powers thereby, and (3) statutory boards—those created by and obtaining their authority from special enactment of the legislature.[5]

These designations, however, actually are not mutually exclusive and therefore are somewhat confusing, especially in the case of "statutory" as opposed to "corporate" boards. The boards which are not established by constitutional authority derive their corporate status, directly or indirectly from the legislature.

In this regard, the observation can be made that many of the terms now in general use to describe the official source of authority of boards of trustees need more precise definition and application. In the writings bearing on college and university administration such terms are found as "chartered," "approved," "accredited," "authorized," and "incorporated."

The term "chartered" generally is used to indicate that a board

---

[5] John H. McNeely, *Higher Education in the Scheme of State Government*, U.S. Office of Education Bulletin No. 3, 1939 (Washington, D.C.: USGPO, 1939), p. 100.

has been authorized by some agency—public or private—to operate a college or university. In chartering the institution, the higher authority sets forth such conditions as it wants to impose and the institution agrees to accept in order to operate within the framework of the higher authority.

"Incorporated" is the term used to signify that the board has legal corporate status; this can be given to it directly in the legal action which created it, or can be acquired by complying with procedures for incorporation set forth in the laws of the several states. These procedures may require the approval of an official state agency, but use of the term "approved" alone is misleading because this expression is used also to refer to matters unrelated to legal incorporation of the board of trustees. Such matters in most instances relate to the acceptability of the institution's academic program and is more in the nature of accreditation.

"Accredited" properly is used to show acceptance or recognition of the institution's academic program of offerings, in whole or in part, by a state agency responsible for making such evaluations officially, by a group of higher institutions voluntarily banding together to guarantee minimum standards of operation, or by a professional association interested in the quality of programs to prepare practitioners in the field. Thus, for example, the State Board of Education in the State of Washington must approve community-junior colleges in order for them to receive state financial aid; the North Central Association of Colleges and Secondary Schools accredits institutions which meet its standards; and the Engineers Council for Professional Development accredits particular curriculums in engineering.

In the sense that their boards of trustees are deemed to be corporate bodies with certain rights and privileges attached to that status and are officially authorized to operate, both publicly and privately controlled higher institutions are chartered. For purposes of this monograph, however, there is merit to discussing the legal bases of authority of boards of trustees of publicly controlled institutions separately from those of colleges which operate under private auspices. This is true for two reasons: (1) among publicly controlled institutions both boards with constitutional and boards with statutory powers are found, and (2) the issue of relative advantages relating to constitutional versus statutory sources of authority is a strong one pertaining to publicly controlled institutions. Among the privately controlled colleges and universities, on the other hand, the issue is virtually nonexistent. Insofar as the author could detetrmine, only two privately controlled higher institutions have provisions bearing upon them in the state constitution in which they are located. The constitutions in Connecticut and Massachusetts confirm the charters that existed in these states for Yale College and Harvard College, respectively, before the founding of the United States. Since almost all the privately controlled colleges derive their authority from the legislatures and from statutory enactments concerning charters and procedures for incorporation these will be discussed separately.

Publicly controlled colleges: constitutional and statutory boards. By far the greater number of publicly controlled higher institutions are under the control of boards which derive authority from state statutes. From Table 2 it is evident that this is true of almost two out of three of the four-year institutions and practically all the two-year colleges. About one in five of the four-year colleges are governed by boards which have some foundation in the state constitution but also rely on state statutes for authority to control the institution. The remaining number, about one out of six of the four-year institutions and one out of thirty of the two-year ones are under clearcut constitutional boards of trustees.

TABLE 2

DISTRIBUTION OF PUBLICLY CONTROLLED HIGHER INSTITUTIONS
CONTROLLED BY CONSTITUTIONAL AND STATUTORY BOARDS, 1959

Source of Authority of Board	Two-Year Colleges *	Four-Year Colleges **	Total
Constitution	13***	54	67
Constitution and Statute	—	69	69
Statute	341	203	544
Total	354	326	680

Source: S. V. Martorana and Ernest V. Hollis, *State Boards Responsible for Higher Education,* augmented by examination of state laws by author.

    * Does not include Hershey Junior College, Pennsylvania, which is quasi private or Panama Canal Zone Junior College which is Federal.

    ** Does not include military academies.

    *** 8 under Georgia Regents of University System and 5 under Oklahoma Board of Regents, A & M Colleges.

Some special significance can perhaps be attached to the relative paucity of boards which have a clear constitutional basis. The boards that can be so designated number only thirty and include, for example, the Regents of the University of California; the Regents of the University of Colorado; the Regents of the University System of Georgia; the Regents of the University of Michigan, Michigan State University, and Wayne State University; the Board of Regents of the University of the State of New York; and the Oklahoma State Regents for Higher Education. Of these thirty boards, eleven govern only a single institution, twelve have multiple institutional units under their jurisdiction, five are State Boards of Education, one (the New York State Regents oversees all education in the state, public and private), and only one (the Oklahoma State Regents for Higher Education) is a board responsible for coordinating functions only.

Some authorities in American higher education contend that distinct advantages accrue to a board of control of a college or university when it has the state constitution as the source of its authority and power. M. M. Chambers, for example, points out with respect to the University of California:

> Created by the legislature in 1868, the Board of Regents was made an independent department of the state by the Constitution of 1879, which perpetuated the "organization and government" of the university. This clause of the Constitution, as construed in several subsequent decisions of the state supreme court, gives the Regents a degree of autonomy somewhat similar to that of the judiciary, and protects the university from over-zealous meddling in its affairs by the legislature or by agencies of the state executive department.[6]

Speaking of the University of Minnesota, this same author observes:

> The Board of Regents of the University of Minnesota is a historic autonomous body whose powers originally conferred by the Territorial legislature were confirmed in the Constitution of 1857. No great attention seems to have been paid to its autonomous status until the notable case of *State v. Chase,* decided by the state supreme court in 1928, sustained the right of the Regents to make lawful

---

[6] M. M. Chambers, *Voluntary Statewide Coordination in Public Higher Education* (Ann Arbor, Mich.: The University of Michigan Press, 1961), p. 10.

disbursements even when disapproved on grounds of policy by the recently-created State Commission of Administration and Finance. Other subsequent decisions have also upheld the autonomy of the Regents in the management of the University.[7]

Michigan is a state which is especially committed historically to providing a constitutional basis for the board of control of its major universities. Constitutional authority for the Regents of the University of Michigan dates back to 1850. A similar recognition in the constitution was given to the Board of Trustees of Michigan State University in 1908 and in 1959 to the Board of Governors of Wayne State University—although with a breadth of powers slightly different from that of the boards of the other two major universities.

Pointing out indirectly the relative degrees of board autonomy possessed by boards with constitutional as opposed to statutory authority, Chambers compares Purdue and Indiana Universities and the state colleges in Indiana with the University of California and those in Michigan. He says:

> None of the institutions has any of the constitutional autonomy such as has the University of California and the principal universities in Michigan. There is no special shield to protect any of these governing boards from the ministrations of the chief state fiscal officers.[8]

Although the record of court decisions resolving legal questions of authority of boards of trustees in the several states clearly shows advantages in favor of a constitutional basis for the board, this advantage hangs on a frail thread. This is because the legislature ultimately controls the budget of state-supported institutions. Although the constitutional protection may be helpful in providing freedom in expenditure of funds that have been provided the institution, it cannot assure that the legislature will provide adequate funds. The former type of protection was stressed by Russell when he wrote:

> The inclusion of the clause concerning control over funds and expenditures has made an important difference in the extent to which the University of Michigan and Michigan State University are subject to regulation by the Legislature and the State fiscal authorities, as compared with the other State-controlled institutions in

---

[7] *Ibid.*, p. 48.
[8] *Ibid.*, p. 25.

Michigan for which the Constitution and the statutes reserve no such rights to the respective boards of control.[9]

The advantages of freedom that a board of trustees has in actual practice must stem from a consistent and traditional practice of legislative support without interference. Freedom with a limited or grudging legislative support may be as deterring to institutional progress in the long run as greater controls accompanied by willing support. Indeed, some institutions whose boards of control have constitutional foundation for their being and their powers have been vexed by both loss of autonomy and inadequate support over long periods of time. For example, the legal source of authority of the Regents of Higher Education in South Dakota dates back to the territorial government and the state constitution of 1896. The wording of the constitution gives substantial powers to the Regents, but there has been nonetheless a history of effort to win legislative support and freedom from executive and legislative controls.[10]

Privately controlled colleges: chartered and incorporated boards. The official or legal source of authority for boards of control of privately controlled colleges and universities is not always as clearly identifiable as it is for those responsible for publicly controlled institutions. This results in part from the fact that some privately controlled colleges date far back to the earliest days of American history and their initial source of legal authority antedates the admission as a state of the area in which the institutions are located. Vagueness of legal authorization in other cases results from the wide variation in requirements among the states whereby higher institutions can be created under private auspices.

An illustration of the first type of difficulty in describing the legal and official source of authority of some privately controlled colleges is seen in the case of the University of Pennsylvania. The legal origins of this institution can be traced to a charitable trust established in 1740 for the stated purpose of providing in Philadelphia a "Charity School and House of Public Worship." Two groups of trustees known respectively as the "Holders of Lands and Buildings" and

---

[9] John Dale Russell, *Higher Education in Michigan,* The Final Report of the Survey of Higher Education in Michigan (Lansing, Mich.: Michigan Legislative Study Committee on Higher Education, 1958), p. 104.

[10] S. V. Martorana, Ernest V. Hollis, and Staff Members of the Division of Higher Education, *Higher Education in South Dakota: A Report of a Survey* (Pierre, S.D.: Legislative Research Council, 1960), pp. 32-38.

"Trustees for Uses" were designated. Litigation between the boards developed later and it was not until 1791 that the status of the institution was stabilized by a merger of the two boards which were then designated as a corporation with its present title. "The Trustees of the University of Pennsylvania." [11]

The Supreme Court of the United States has ruled that charters granted by the states to privately controlled institutions of higher learning are of the same character as charters of private corporations; they are contracts between the legislature and the corporations and as such are protected under Article 1, Section 10 of the Constitution of the United States. Under this ruling, the right of an educational institution to exist as a private corporation was upheld in the famous Dartmouth College case.[12] Dartmouth College is a privately controlled institution originally established in 1769 by a charter granted by the King of Great Britain. In 1816, the New Hampshire Legislature attempted to void this charter and create a new public corporation. The following statement from judgment of the Supreme Court on February 2, 1819, shows the issues that were considered and the way the ruling in favor of the College assured the future legal status of privately controlled colleges:

> That education is an object of national concern, and a proper subject of legislation, all admit. That there may be an institution, founded by government, and placed entirely under its immediate control, the officers of which would be public officers, amenable exclusively to government, none will deny. But is Dartmouth College such an institution? Is education altogether in the hands of government? Does every teacher of youth become a public officer, and do donations for the purpose of education necessarily become public property, so far that the will of the legislature, not the will of the donor, becomes the law of the donation? These questions are of serious moment to society, and deserve to be well considered.[13]

It is interesting to note that the Supreme Court in the Dartmouth College case upheld the rights of the privately controlled institution that stemmed originally from a source other than the state legislature itself. As has been stated above, the usual source of

---

[11] Donald R. Belcher, *The Board of Trustees of the University of Pennsylvania* (Philadelphia: The University of Pennsylvania Press, 1960), pp. 15-17.

[12] *Dartmouth College v. Woodward,* United States Reports, Wheaton 4, pp. 310-11.

[13] *Ibid.,* pp. 302-3.

authority for a college board of trustees is the legislature of the state in which the institution operates. This is the general case, not the universal rule. In some instances the college is established as part of a larger social organization other than or in addition to the state in which it is located and in such instances derives its authority really from two sources. To operate within the framework of purposes and structure of the larger nonstate social organization, the institution must be chartered by the larger body. If the state requires, the institution will also have to seek the official recognition and incorporation legally.

The fact that the church-related colleges must seek in effect two charters is the principal differentiation between this class of colleges and the independent, privately controlled higher institutions. An excellent statement on the internal and external controls on Catholic colleges was given by Tasch in 1946.[14] In it he reports that in a survey of 50 Catholic colleges and universities, the following types of organizational and administrative setup were found:

> (1) The Religious Corporation is the parent corporation and owns the property and facilities used by the college. (2) There is but one corporation, the Religious, which conducts the colleges as one of its activities. (3) The Religious Corporation or community, in all cases, furnishes most of the personnel, administration and faculty, for the college. (4) Religious Superiors constitute the board of trustees, either entirely or in majority ratio. (5) Religious Superiors exercise their canonical prerogative of disposition of their subjects in the matter of appointments. (6) Religious corporations and/or religious Superiors exercise certain financial controls below the limits set by Canon Law for the Holy See. (7) The President may also be the religious Superior, local or major.

Another study reported that even when chosen members of the community or parent corporation form a separate corporation for the conduct of a college, they must obtain authorization for the original extent of activities in accordance with religious statutes.[15] Thus, for example, the Catholic University of America states in

---

[14] Alcuin W. Tasch, "Organization and Statutes," in *College Organization and Administration* (The Proceedings of the Workshop on College Organization and Administration, conducted at the Catholic University of America from June 17-June 27, 1946), Roy J. Deferrari, ed. (Washington, D.C.: The Catholic University of America Press, 1947), pp. 61-64.

[15] "Corporate Entities." Unpublished paper presented by Rev. Vitus Kriegel at St. Vincent College, Latrobe, Pa., 1945.

American Universities and Colleges that it was incorporated in 1887 but chartered by Pope Leo XIII in 1889.[16] By virtue of its charter and articles of incorporation, recognition is given by the Roman Catholic Church and the District of Columbia—respectively—to the "board of trustees of 36 members, composed of the cardinals and bishops of the United States, and, in addition, not more than thirty other members elected from bishops, priests, and laymen" and power is granted to the board to govern the institution within the two frameworks of authority. Similarly, Our Lady of the Lake College in San Antonio, Texas, which has a "self-perpetuating board of lay trustees of 18 members," reports that it was chartered in 1896 by "the Congregation of the Sisters of Divine Providence." [17]

These two illustrations should not lead to a conclusion that only colleges related to the Roman Catholic Church view themselves as chartered by the church or subgroups within it. Examination of charters of church-related colleges affiliated with other denominations often shows similar official relationships between the institution and the church body concerned. The board of MacMurray College in Illinois, for example, holds property and received its powers "under the patronage and control of the Illinois Annual Conference of the Methodist Episcopal Church." [18] In many church-related institutions, the trustees are elected from candidates nominated by the church body or subgroup.

It is apparent then that the acquisition of a charter can be and often is different from the act of incorporation. Incorporation represents legal designation of the board of trustees as "a body corporate" and a fulfillment of the conditions required of a "corporation" to operate in a particular state. Often both the acquisition of a charter and the incorporation of the board are accomplished in a single legal step, but this is not always the case.

Beach and Will point out that the state may regulate privately controlled educational institutions through its system of incorporation. These authors also report that incorporation is a facility rather than a requirement, stating that "it is rarely required of educational institutions other than institutions of higher education conferring

---

16 *American Universities and Colleges, 1960,* 8th ed. (Washington, D.C.: American Council on Education, 1960), p. 275.

17 *American Universities and Colleges, op. cit.,* p. 1010.

18 The Charter of MacMurray College, Ill., as amended on June 19, 1953, p. 1.

degrees." [19] With respect to institutions of higher education, however, the practice is universal among the fifty states although the procedures required for compliance vary greatly. Whatever the procedures are, the two chief matters dealt with usually are the purpose of the institution and the composition of the board of trustees. In a detailed study of the basic documents of government of twelve institutions, graduate students of the Catholic University found the purpose and governing body of the institution to be the subjects most often stipulated.[20]

In the earlier years privately controlled bodies wishing to establish a college or university would seek a charter directly from the state legislature. The charter would outline the character of the controlling board and the plan of self-government and operation of the institution. With the increase of legislative responsibilities in the states, however, this historical practice became progressively more difficult to maintain. The procedure, besides being difficult to manage, allowed unilateral bargaining with the legislature with resulting exposure of this body to possible pressures and requests from groups seeking charters. As a result, the procedure changed gradually: general laws governing incorporation were enacted and state agencies to administer these laws were formed. This trend toward general legislative provisions has been strengthened in recent years by the creation of statewide agencies responsible for higher education.

In most of the states with statewide coordinating boards responsible for higher education, the approval of this agency must be obtained before a college can be incorporated. The actual incorporating authority in most states, however, is a noneducational governmental agency, usually the Secretary of State. Only in New York State is an educational agency. The Regents of the University of New York, fully authorized to incorporate a privately controlled institution.

Several other states require the approval of proposed articles of incorporation or amendments to charters before the incorporating authority of the state may grant or amend charters. To cite just two

[19] Fred F. Beach and Robert F. Will, *The State and Nonpublic Schools, With Particular Reference to Responsibility of State Departments of Education,* U.S. Office of Education (Washington, D.C.: USGPO, 1958), p. 9.

[20] "Historical Appraisal of American Colleges and University Fundamentals of Government." Unpublished study by Dr. George F. Donovan, *et al.,* presented at The Catholic University of America, Washington, D.C., January 15, 1962.

examples, in Arkansas "persons desiring to become a corporation as trustees of a college or university or other institution of learning" must obtain a certificate from the state board of education approving their plan before a charter of incorporation may be filed and recorded by the secretary of state. In Rhode Island each "academy, college, university or other institution of secondary or higher education" seeking to be incorporated must have its application approved by the state board of education before a charter may be granted. Other illustrations can be found in Illinois, Massachusetts, Pennsylvania, Vermont, and West Virginia.

To gain insight into the source of legal authority cited by privately controlled colleges and universities for their operation, the author tabulated the citations of authority given by such institutions in the volumes, *American Universities and Colleges, 1960,* and *American Junior Colleges, 1960,* both published by the American Council on Education. The results are shown in Table 3. Admittedly the data presented in these reference volumes are fragmentary. Nonetheless, at least one striking fact emerges from the tabulation: a large number of privately controlled institutions do not report any source of legal authority for the board of control and the operation of the institution.

TABLE 3

SOURCES OF BOARD AUTHORITY CITED BY PRIVATELY
CONTROLLED HIGHER INSTITUTIONS, 1960

Source of Authority of Board	Two-Year Colleges	Four-Year Colleges	Total
Charter	72	424	496
Articles of Incorporation	56	131	187
Not Specified	106	181	287
Total	234	736*	970

Source: Tabulation by author from *American Colleges and Universities, 1960* and *American Junior Colleges, 1960.* Washington, D.C.: American Council on Education, 1961.

   * Includes 35 institutions which reported *both* charter and articles of incorporation; does not include 4 institutons which cited other sources.

Four out of five of the privately controlled junior colleges and approximately one out of four of the four-year institutions did not indicate the legal basis of operation. The more recent history of the two-year college movement is reflected in the fact that a significantly larger proportion—about one in four—of these institutions (as compared with four-year colleges) report that they are incorporated. In contrast, some six out of ten of the four-year colleges report that they are chartered institutions.

The study of the institutional exhibits of the privately controlled colleges and universities not only brought out the varied practice in reporting the legal basis of the institution, but also led to several other observations pertinent to boards of trustees. One that already has been mentioned is the fact that the acquisition of a charter is not always synonymous with incorporation. Relatively few institutions report that they are both chartered and incorporated. This suggests that the terms "chartered" and "incorporated" may be used somewhat interchangeably by the persons making the reports for the institutions. Although such a conclusion cannot be reached firmly on the basis of the data analyzed, it is reinforced by the fact that colleges reporting from the same state sometimes use the two terms but do not report both types of authorization for a given institution. To illustrate, of the 44 privately controlled four-year institutions in California included in *American Universities and Colleges, 1960,* 22 report that they are chartered, 15 that they are incorporated, nine do not specify their legal basis, and two claim both chartered and incorporated status.

Another interesting observation on this subject is the apparent transferability of authority of a charter for operation of a particular type of educational institution from one board to the same board or other boards for operation of other types of educational institutions. That this has proved true can in many cases be inferred from the statements of the history of the institutions and references to charters or articles of incorporation. Illustrations of such experiences are found in the histories of Duke University, which was founded as Union Institute but at one time was reorganized as a Normal College to train teachers for state public schools; Hofstra College, which started off as an extension of New York University; and Maryville College of the Sacred Heart in Missouri, which was first established as a convent and started offering programs of higher education as a junior college.

CHAPTER III

Characteristics of Boards of Trustees

In view of the deep public trust placed in persons who serve on boards of trustees, one would expect that they as persons and as groups would be the subject of many scholarly studies. Contrary to this expectation, relatively few definitive studies of characteristics of boards of trustees are to be found in the published writings on higher education. This remains an area in which research is yet in the pioneering stage, despite the fact that colleges and universities have been operating for over three hundred years.

Among the earliest attempts to relate objectively the characteristics of boards of trustees to excellence of institutions was that made by the Committee on Revision of Standards of the Commission on Higher Institutions of the North Central Association of Colleges and Secondary Schools. From this study several items referring to boards of trustees were identified as having an influence in establishing institutional excellence. They were: (1) length of terms of board membership, (2) provisions for overlapping of terms of board membership, (3) occupational distribution of board membership, (4) avoidance of board members on the salaried staff of the institution, and (5) functions performed by the board and board committees.[1]

Several factors which might have been included but which were specifically omitted from the list derived by the North Central Association's Committee are significant because of their relation to later studies of board characteristics. The list of items found not to have a significant relation to institutional excellence were: (1) number of members on the board, (2) method of selecting members, (3) number and kinds of committees, (4) frequency of regular meetings, (5) attendance at board meetings, (6) residence of members, and (7) ages of members.[2]

It is interesting to compare these two groupings of topics with those found in another more recent study which also used statistical

---

[1] John Dale Russell and Floyd W. Reeves, *The Evaluation of Higher Institutions* (Chicago: The University of Chicago Press, 1936), pp. 18-27.

[2] *Ibid.*, p. 29.

approaches to data analysis but examined the attributes of "good" versus "bad" motivation for membership and related effectiveness of members of boards of lower public schools. This found that such factors as sex, marital status, education, age (except after 65), income and occupation were not significantly related to "good" board motivation. However, such motivation was significantly related to having children in school, residence, and involvement in politics— the first two carrying a positive relationship and the third a negative one.[3]

The North Central Association's study was aimed at using the board as an approach to evaluating the institution and stressed objective attributes of boards. In contrast, a more recent study was aimed at learning the qualities of boards that do not lend themselves to statistical determination or measurement. From this inquiry came the conclusion:

> The unique characteristics, then, of American boards are that: (1) they are composed of laymen; (2) they are invested with complete power of management, most of which they delegate to professional educators; (3) they operate without the checks and balances typical of our democratic society.[4]

It appears from the studies just quoted as well as from the findings of others that, though they are interrelated, board characteristics and board operations should be discussed separately. Except for a few factors, evidence to relate objectively the one topic to the other is lacking. This chapter, therefore, will report on characteristics of boards: qualifications, methods of selection, terms of office and tenure, and size. The next chapter will discuss the matter of board organization and board operations in relation to the institutions for which they are responsible.

Qualifications of Board Members

The attributes looked for among board members can be identified through several approaches. One is the statements regarding the composition of boards of trustees that appear in the documents founding colleges and universities—that is, state constitutions, stat-

---

[3] Neal Gross, *Who Runs Our Schools* (New York: John Wiley and Sons, 1958), pp. 77-86.

[4] Morton A. Rauh, *College and University Trusteeship* (Yellow Springs, Ohio: The Antioch Press, 1959), p. 15.

utes, charters, and articles of incorporation. Another would be the public discourses and scholarly writings that are related to this subject. Still another would be by examination of the actual membership of boards of trustees. Studies which have used these approaches separately or in combination are mentioned in the discussion which follows.

Legally prescribed qualifications. To this writer's knowledge no thoroughly analytical study has yet been made of the legally prescribed qualifications for membership on boards of trustees of both publicly and privately controlled institutions of higher learning. Yet there often exist in the legislation relating to public institutions and in the charters and articles of incorporation of private ones stipulations of requirements for board membership. Beck, in his chapter on "Qualifications Recommended for University Governing Board Members" makes an extensive review of the literature to 1947,[5] and points out the qualifications believed to be most often mentioned in basic charters and legislation. Beck concludes that the qualifications most frequently found in the legal documents of higher institutions are occupation, age, sex, religion, and residence. He calls attention to the fact that a stipulation regarding religion was found only with reference to privately controlled institutions; in this group it is a frequent requirement. On the other hand, Beck concludes that legal requirements of such qualifications as personality and ideals, wealth and income, politics, education, and family connections do not exist. In some cases, however, there is a requirement that all or a part of the board membership must be alumni of the institution.[6]

Among the special requirements for members of 209 state boards responsible for publicly controlled higher institutions, Martorana and Hollis found the residence requirement to be the most frequently stipulated, 111 boards having this requisite for membership. Generally, this means that a member must be a qualified voter, sometimes of a state, sometimes of a county, and sometimes of a congressional district; also, often, a minimum period of citizenship is specified. Concern over the political composition of the boards of publicly controlled institutions is apparent in the finding that 44 boards required that their composition be bipartisan. Among the

---

[5] Hubert Park Beck, *Men Who Control Our Universities* (New York: King's Crown Press, 1947), pp. 35-46.

[6] *Ibid.,* p. 44.

other required elements in the makeup of boards found worthy of note in this study were the setting of minimum or maximum ages, presence of one or more almuni among the membership, occupation of some members, reservation of one or more memberships to women, and guarantees that the board would be made up of lay personnel.[7]

Attributes of membership beyond legal prescription.   Much has been written and many discourses have been held on the subject of the "ideal trustee." Many of these idealize the personage of the trustee. Almost thirty years ago, three scholars of college administration drew upon writings from eight sources to reach these conclusions as to the types of persons who should be elected to boards of trustees:

> Those who are free from the dominance of any partisan group; conversant with history and ideals of the institution; leaders in their own special fields of activity so that the public has confidence in their ability; able and willing to devote considerable time to their duties; and capable of regarding higher education as a dynamic force in civilization and their trusteeship as a high form of civic service.[8]

Two of the eight sources used were statements made at the 1924 meeting of the Association of Governing Boards of State Universities and Allied Institutions.[9] For many years that organization has worked to develop a better understanding of the qualities expected in an effective member of a board of trustees. Every year much attention is given to the proper role and best traits of trustees. In one of its most recent publications, for example, the trustee's function was termed "A Citizen's Highest Functions," the title of a five-point creed for new trustees.[10]

The fact remains, however, that relatively little effort has been extended to examine analytically the actual membership of boards of

[7] S. V. Martorana and Ernest V. Hollis, *State Boards Responsible for Higher Education,* U.S. Office of Education Circular OE-53005 (Washington, D.C.: USGPO, 1960), pp. 30-31.

[8] Edward C. Elliott, M. M. Chambers, and William A. Ashbrook, *The Government of Higher Education* (New York: American Book Company, 1935), p. 42.

[9] James W. Fessler, "The Functions of Boards of Trustees," *Proceedings,* Association of Governing Boards of State Universities and Allied Institutions, 1924, pp. 56-60; and Junius E. Beal, *Ibid.,* pp. 65-69.

[10] Milton W. Durham, "A Citizen's Highest Responsibility," *Proceedings,* Association of Governing Boards of State Universities and Allied Institutions, October 19-22, 1960, pp. 82-84.

trustees in terms of the standards expected of such membership. Summarizing his definitive study of this question as it pertained to thirty leading universities, Beck pointed out several important generalizations. One of these was that practically 90 percent of the trustees formerly had been college students and thus had developed some measure of close understanding of higher education. Membership of the boards he studied showed a very high proportion of leaders of "large-scale business and finance," though lower among the publicly controlled institutions than among the privately controlled ones. His findings with respect to age level suggested that this was too high, 47 percent were over 60 years of age and 18 percent were 70 or over. The proportion of women on these boards, however, was very low—less than 5 percent. Finally, Beck observed that the trustees he studied were generally of a conservative political and social orientation. These findings, he concluded, would provide support for those who argued that boards should be made up of persons with knowledge of higher education, and individuals who have themselves achieved positions of status and leadership. The findings, however, show violation of the principles that members of these boards should be of different viewpoint, background, sex, and age.[11]

On one of the qualifications agreement of writers in the field appears to be overwhelming. This is the expectation that persons selected for membership on boards of trustees will have and will take the time to devote to their duties. The emphasis on the importance of the time of trustees comes up repeatedly and in many ways. In one of the documents of the Middle States Association of Colleges and Secondary Schools, for example, appears the caution:

> Good trustees undertake their office with a sense of responsibility and readiness to take enough time to study and understand educational problems and practices and to become acquainted with their own institution in more than a superficial way. Lack of time, or failure to take enough time for the work is often the reason why a trustee proves inadequate.[12]

The admonition that time is needed to do justice to all responsibilities can also be directed to entire boards as well as to individuals.

---

[11] Beck, *op. cit.*, pp. 128-33.

[12] *Junior Colleges and Community Colleges,* Middle States Association of Colleges and Secondary Schools, Document No. 4 (New York: The Association, December, 1958), p. 60.

In those instances when a given board is responsible for more than one institution—as in the case of a governing-coordinating board —or of more than one level of education, boards sometimes fail to do justice to all aspects of their assignment. To this point, the declaration of the President of the California Junior College Faculty Association in 1961 has meaning. He said: "Many California school boards today devote 98 percent of their time to elementary and secondary problems and give only 2 percent of their time to junior college problems." [13] Nor is the feeling strong only with regard to members of boards of trustees responsible for two-year colleges. A. C. Wilgrus was referring to those on boards of four-year colleges and universities when he concluded that the main reason why the average trustee often fails to acquaint himself sufficiently with the institution and its affairs to be a good builder of policies for its government is lack of time.[14] Capen directed attention of trustees of urban unversities to the same possibility when he said:

> It is not an easy job to be a trustee of this type of institution. It makes large demands on the time of many members of the board. It requires imagination and the occasional exercise of moral courage. No reward is attached to the job, except the consciousness of having performed an important public service.[15]

Methods of Selection

There are four ways whereby persons are selected for membership on boards of trustees: (1) election, (2) appointment, (3) co-optation, and (4) *ex officio* selection. Under procedures followed for election of board members, either the entire constituency of a college or university or large segments of the constituency indicate their choice of persons to serve on the board of trustees. The appointment procedure places control of selection of board members in the hands of one official or a small group of officials among the constituency of the institution—for example, the governor of a state or the head of a denominational church group. By co-optation is meant that the board members themselves retain the right and duty at any given

---

[13] John Palmer, *Bulletin of the California Junior College Faculty Association,* IV (December, 1961), No. 12, 5.

[14] A. C. Wilgrus, "Too Trustful Trustees," *School and Society,* LII (August 24, 1940), 126-28.

[15] Samuel P. Capen, *The Management of Universities* (Buffalo, N.Y.: Foster and Stewart Publishing Corporation, 1953), pp. 36-37.

time of selecting persons to fill vacancies or to add to the board membership. *Ex officio* members, as the term indicates, are determined automatically by virtue of a particular office held by the person.

Other writers identify additional ways that board members are selected. Beck, for instance, lists six methods of selection of the board members of the institutions he studied.[16] Actually, however, these were refinements or extensions of the main procedures enumerated above. Table 4, taken from a recent analysis by Walter Crosby Eells, tabulates the number of baccalaureate degree-granting institutions which follow various practices in the selection of the majority membership of the boards of trustees.

Both Eells's study and Beck's show that the prevailing method of selecting board members among privately controlled institutions is by co-optation and that among publicly controlled colleges the modal practice is the use of appointment by elected state officials.[17] The same conclusion about the publicly controlled institutions was reached in the 1959 study of 209 state boards. This study, in contrast to those by Eells and Beck, analyzes selection procedures in relation to the duties of the board. It was found that governing boards had the highest proportion of appointed members—more than three out of four of the members were selected in this fashion. The official making the appointment of trustees to boards of publicly controlled institutions is usually the governor. Almost 70 percent of board members were found to be appointed by joint action of the governor and senate and more than 25 percent by that of the governor alone. Only in the case of the "other" boards in this study were more members observed to be selected by direct action of the governor than were appointed by him with approval of the state senate. More memberships were determined by election among governing-coordinating and "other" boards than among those classified strictly as governing boards or as coordinating boards. This is because a large number of the governing-coordinating and "other" boards were state boards of education, a type of board where election of members by popular vote is a common practice.[18]

This same study made a comparison of its data with regard to the

---

16 Beck, *op. cit.*, p. 116.
17 *Ibid.*, p. 197.
18 Martorana and Hollis, *op. cit.*, pp. 26-27.

TABLE 4—Distribution of American Universities and Colleges, 1960, According to Methods of Selection of Majority of Members of Boards of Control

Method	Grand Total of Institutions	Public — Total	Federal	State	Municipal	Private — Total	Nonsectarian	Roman Catholic	Protestant Denominations — Total	Methodist	Presbyterian	Baptist	Lutheran	United Church of Christ	Disciples	7th-Day Adventist	Others
Total	1,046	340	6	318	16	706	191	199	316	80	63	49	29	21	12	10	52
Elected or appointed by church body	326	—	—	—	—	326	—	117	209	64	39	29	24	7	5	7	34
Self-perpetuating	271	5	—	3	2	266	156	28	82	8	23	13	4	13	6	—	15
Appointed by governor	108	108	—	108	—	—	—	—	—	—	—	—	—	—	—	—	—
Appointed by governor, with confirmation by senate	168	168	—	168	—	—	—	—	—	—	—	—	—	—	—	—	—
Appointed by governor, with confirmation by legislature	8	8	—	8	—	—	—	—	—	—	—	—	—	—	—	—	—
Elected by voters	21	21	—	20	1	—	—	—	—	—	—	—	—	—	—	—	—
Elected by corporation	21	—	—	—	—	21	16	3	2	—	—	—	1	—	—	—	1
Appointed by mayor	9	9	—	—	9	—	—	—	—	—	—	—	—	—	—	—	—
Elected by legislature	8	8	—	8	—	—	—	—	—	—	—	—	—	—	—	—	—
Appointed by president of institution	5	—	—	—	—	5	—	5	—	—	—	—	—	—	—	—	—
Appointed by federal department	3	3	3	—	—	—	—	—	—	—	—	—	—	—	—	—	—
Other methods **	4	4	—	—	4	—	—	—	—	—	—	—	—	—	—	—	—
No information	94	6	3	3	—	88	19	46	23	8	1	7	—	1	1	3	2
Ex officio																	
State superintendent of public instruction	124	120	—	120	—	4	4	—	—	—	—	—	—	—	—	—	—
President of institution	101	12	3	9	—	89	34	22	33	14	6	2	2	1	—	1	7
Church official	52	—	—	—	—	52	—	29	23	12	—	—	4	—	—	1	6
Governor	40	31	—	31	—	9	8	—	1	1	—	—	—	—	—	—	—
Mayor	13	4	—	2	2	9	2	4	3	1	—	—	1	—	—	—	1
President of alumni association	9	4	—	4	—	5	3	—	2	1	—	—	—	—	—	—	1
Others †	47	28	—	24	4	19	13	—	3	1	1	—	—	—	1	1	—
Individual not specified	32	14	—	14	—	18	2	6	10	4	—	—	2	—	—	—	4

Source: Walter Crosby Eells, "Boards of Control of Universities and Colleges," *The Educational Record*, XLII (October, 1961), 338.

** Appointed by U.S. District Court judge, by city board of education, by city commission and board of education.

† *State*: secretary of state, attorney general, adjutant general, director of finance, commissioner of agriculture, secretary of mines, president-board of agriculture and immigration, chairmen of education, committees of state senate and house, president-state board of education, master of state grange, all living ex-governors. *Nonsectarian*: vice-president, deans, treasurer, lieutenant-governor, speakers of state senate and house, city superintendent of schools, city librarian, president of city YMCA. *Catholic*: cardinals, archbishops, deans, registrar, treasurer. *Protestant*: dean, business manager.

42

number of persons who held membership in an *ex officio* capacity on boards that had been created between 1950 and 1959. The comparison showed a slight increase in elected and *ex officio* membership and a slight decrease in appointed members. Of the 26 boards created between 1950 and 1959, half had at least one *ex officio* member serving on the board.[19] Among the 209 boards, the state superintendent of public instruction held *ex officio* membership most frequently, with the governor and president of the institution next in frequency. The superintendent was found on all types of boards, but most often on governing boards where the governor of the state was also most frequently observed. No coordinating board had the governor as a member. A college president was found among the membership of one or more boards of all types but most often on governing boards.

The practice of having *ex officio* members of the board of trustees is not restricted to those responsible for public higher institutions. It is a strikingly common practice among privately controlled institutions. Eells's data, reported in Table 4, show that 205 of the 706 boards of privately controlled institutions had *ex officio* members. Most often these are the presidents of the colleges or church officials. Some of the officials who hold such memberships by virtue of the public offices they hold. The institutional exhibits reported in *American Colleges and Universities* bring out such illustrations as the state governors serving *ex officio* on the boards of Dartmouth, Princeton, and the University of Pennsylvania, and the Governor of Louisiana and the Mayor of New Orleans on the board of Tulane.

In view of the relatively frequent practice of having a church official hold an *ex officio* membership on the boards of colleges related to the Roman Catholic Church, the following statement concerning the selection of board members in such institutions is noteworthy:

> Membership may be determined according to charter provisions (a) by co-optation, if the charter empowers it to perpetuate itself by filling vacancies due to death, resignation, removal or retirement; (b) by appointment through ecclesiastical or religious superiors; (c) *ex officio*. Corporation law permits such membership, but in the interest of stability there should be as few *ex officio* members as possible.[20]

---

[19] *Ibid.*, pp. 26-27.
[20] Alcuin W. Tasch, *op. cit.*, pp. 65-66.

Making the president of the institution a member of the board of trustees in an *ex officio* capacity may be viewed as compounding error. Eells states the danger succinctly when he says:

> In a certain sense this is an anomaly, since theoretically the function of the board of control is to determine institutional policies, while the president is the executive officer who carries them out. One of the chief functions of the board is to select the president of the institution. In most institutions, the president regularly meets with the board but is not himself a voting member of it. This is usually considered the better administrative practice.[21]

Advantages and disadvantages of different methods of selection. The technique whereby persons are selected to serve on boards of trustees is a means to two ends, both of which bear meaningfully on the operating effectiveness of the total board. The goals sought are, first, the identification and procurement of persons best qualified for the job of trustee, and, second, assurance that the membership of the board will exhibit breadth of view and experience and represent well the college constituency. The writings on higher education report general dissatisfaction with present methods of selection in accomplishing these two objectives.

This is not to say that present board members or the boards themselves are held in general disregard. Quite the contrary: the literature is replete with words of praise and appreciation of their service. The attitude reflected in the discussion is more nearly one that disclaims an expected relationship between the way that board members are selected and the quality of the board membership that results. At the start of this chapter note was made that Russell and Reeves did not recommend inclusion of the technique of selecting board members among factors for accrediting institutions of higher learning. Russell in a more recent writing supported the same view from a later and different base of evidence. He wrote of Michigan where both election and appointment of members of boards of public institutions is used:

> A review of the evidence in the State of Michigan yields no evidence that one method of selecting board members is consistently superior to the other. Both methods have resulted in the choice of

---

[21] Walter Crosby Eells, "Boards of Control of Universities and Colleges," *The Educational Record,* XLII (October, 1961), 336-42.

board members who have rendered excellent service to the State and its educational institutions.[22]

Others, however, have questioned the methods of selection that are now in use. The contention is that these methods cause the board memberships to be representative neither of the general constituency served nor of the institution itself. Capen, for example, asserts that:

> It is a simon pure example of authoritarian government. Except in those state institutions whose boards are either popularly elected or appointed by the governor, the controlling body does not directly represent the public or any identifiable group of citizens. In no instance is it representative of the persons who make up the institution: the teachers and the students.[23]

Some interesting contradictions appear on the points where lack of representation is most critical. Capen, in the same work quoted above contends that "The government is also absentee government, since most members of most boards do not reside in the community in which the institution is located." Another writer earlier explored the fact that from his observation the board memberships, especially of small colleges, are often overbalanced by trustees from the local area.[24]

It has even been argued that, regardless of the technical and legally prescribed ways that members are selected, boards are largely *de facto* self-perpetuating in character because of the influence and positions of status held by persons already on the boards.[25] Whatever the point of departure may be, it can be reported that most scholars in the field agree with Eggertson to the point that "selection of trustees from a single social class is an anachronism." [26] Moreover, the weight of authoritative opinion appears to favor for state controlled colleges the appointment method of selecting board membership with the power of appointment held by the governor of the

---

[22] John Dale Russell, *Higher Education in Michigan,* Final Report of the Survey of Higher Education in Michigan (Lansing, Mich.: Legislative Study Committee on Higher Education, September, 1958), p. 105.

[23] Samuel P. Capen, *op. cit.,* p. 7.

[24] H. C. Jaquith, "Are You a Trustee of Education," *Journal of Higher Education,* IX (April, 1938), 197-200.

[25] H. N. Snyder, "College Trustees and College Finances," *Association of American Colleges Bulletin,* XXIV (December, 1938), 459-63.

[26] C. A. Eggertson, "Composition of Governing Boards," John Dewey Society, Tenth Yearbook (Columbus: The Ohio State University), pp. 117-26.

state with confirmation by the senate. Safeguards against political considerations are easier to establish than when popular election is used. Russell put the danger in the latter method subtly when he said:

> The argument is that many citizens who would render outstanding service as members of a college or university board have not identified themselves sufficiently with the activities of one of the major political parties to win the necessary nomination in the State convention prior to being placed on the ballot. Such citizens can be readily considered by the Governor in making appointments to boards, and they are likely to win confirmation by the Senate without regard to party affiliation.[27]

Presumably the same logic would support a parallel scheme for selection of board members for privately controlled institutions. Among the colleges and universities related to Protestant denominations, however, the general practice is to have either all or a majority of the board members elected by the membership of the denomination or a legislative group representative of the entire denomination. Among the independent, privately controlled institutions, co-optation or self-perpetuation are practices which appear to be firmly fixed and continue largely unchallenged. Among those institutions related to the Roman Catholic Church, appointment by official groups in particular religious orders or communities is established practice.

Of the several methods whereby board members are selected, that of designating persons *ex officio* appears to draw greatest criticism from scholars in college administration. This is particularly true when the *ex officio* member is not a voting member. In such cases, strong consensus is found with the conclusion stated by Russell that such membership is ". . . largely window-dressing and serves no real purpose." [28] Several arguments can be advanced against the use of *ex officio* membership on boards of trustees, among them: (1) these persons are extremely busy with other official duties and therefore their ability to devote full time and energy to the higher education board is impaired; (2) such memberships either impede development of broad board representativeness or make it necessary to enlarge the total number on the board, thus contributing to problems

27 John Dale Russell, *op. cit.*, p. 105.
28 *Ibid.*, p. 106.

of manageability; and (3) other techniques for coordinating the business of the board of trustees with that of other official agencies besides *ex officio* membership can be used effectively to gain the desired exchange of views and information.

Chapter II noted that most publicly controlled two-year colleges are authorized by general enabling statutes, authorizing local jurisdictions such as school districts or cities to establish and operate such institutions. Such local public two-year colleges almost universally follow the practice of selecting members of the board of trustees by popular vote. Thus, this group of institutions is set apart from both the large majority of other publicly controlled colleges and the privately controlled four-year and two-year colleges. Privately controlled two-year colleges in general do not differ in any significant way from privately controlled four-year colleges in the practice they follow in choosing trustees.

Tenure of Members

To have continuity and consistency in providing educational services to its constituency, a college or university must have stability in its administrative structure as well as in its program. Because the final authority for decisions on policies which govern both structure and program of the institution rests in the board of trustees, the stability of this body affects the stability of the entire institution.

Regulations governing the terms of office of members of boards of trustees, their rights and duties as members, and protection of their membership are intended to achieve stability for the institution, and for this reason tenure is usually reviewed critically in the accreditation of higher institutions. Evidence is strong in both the legally prescribed conditions bearing on tenure and the actual experience of membership on boards that the stated objective has been generally attained. Drastic upheavals of membership of boards of trustees have occurred, to be sure. But, historically, these have been exceptions rather than the rule in American higher education. No indication of any change in practice is evident.

The legally prescribed terms of office of board members have been examined in several studies. Table 5, from Eells's analysis of institutional reports of board composition shows the terms of office of the majority of board members of colleges and universities granting

TABLE 5

DISTRIBUTION OF AMERICAN UNIVERSITIES AND COLLEGES, 1960, ACCORDING TO TERMS OF OFFICE OF MAJORITY OF MEMBERS OF BOARDS OF CONTROL.

Term of Office	Grand Total of Institutions	Public — Total	Federal	State	Municipal	Private — Total	Nonsectarian	Roman Catholic	Protestant Denominations — Total	Methodist	Presbyterian	Baptist	Lutheran	United Church of Christ	Disciples	7th-Day Adventist	Others
Total	1,046	340	6	318	16	706	191	199	316	80	63	49	29	21	12	10	52
1 year	22	3		2	1	19		17	2			1					1
2 years	9	4		3	1	5	1	2	2							2	13
3 years	221	46		44	2	175	48	19	108	21	25	28	10	6	5		3
4 years	62	20		19	1	42	10		32	8	6	5	5	2	1	4	9
5 years	175	117		114	3	58	26	6	26	2	4	6	2	2	1	2	5
6 years	78	18		18		60	10	29	21	4	4		3		1		
7 years	21	15		15		6	6										
8 years	44	38		33	5	6	4		2	2			1				
9 years	18	16		16		2	1		1		1						
10 years	15	10		10		5	3	1	1								
12 years	1	1		1													
14 years	1	1		1													
16 years																	
Indefinite or not specified	379	51	6	42	3	328	82	125	121	43	23	9	8	11	4	2	21
Percent with definite terms	64	85	0	87	81	54	57	37	62	46	53	80	72	48	67	80	60
Median years for those with definite terms	5	6	—	6	6	3	4	3	3	3	3	3	4	3	3	4	4

Source: Walter Crosby Eells, "Boards of Control of Universities and Colleges," *The Educational Record*, XLII (October, 1961), 341.

baccalaureate degrees. The range shown in length of term is from one year to an indefinite authorization, but the median number of years for members with definite terms ranges from three to six. The study did not report how memberships are staggered to assure continuity in board composition.

From other studies, however, the general practice of providing overlapping terms of office is clear. This practice is strongly advocated and rests on the basic principle that guarantees are needed against removal or replacement of a majority of the board at any one time or by any one official or political group. Of the 209 boards responsible for publicly supported higher institutions in *State Boards Responsible for Higher Education,* 179 reported that members were named for overlapping terms.[29]

Both this study and that by Beck attempted to relate the actual tenure of board members with the stipulated length of a single term of office. The conclusion from both studies was that actually board members serve much longer than the number of years specified for one term. This is made possible because many boards allow members succeed themselves; 185 of the 188 boards which provided information on this subject reported that it was both allowable and the prevalent practice to have board members succeed themselves. The average number of years served on these boards was seven.[30] Beck carried the analysis to the point of relating length of tenure to the occupations of board members. He reported that longest service was held by judges, with a median of fifteen years and the shortest by homemakers, with a median of three years. In between came manufacturers, insurance officials, bankers and financiers, and headmasters,[31] in that order.

Although the prescribed terms of office are for relatively lengthy periods and the record of actual tenure is complementary with respect to stability of boards, the possibility that members can be removed on a whimsical or capricious basis exists for many boards. Dangers that lie in the summary removal of board members of state universities were clearly pointed out by Chambers by reference to several cases of flagrant abuse of the removal power. He concluded

---

[29] Martorana and Hollis, *op. cit.,* Table 7, pp. 227-33.
[30] *Ibid.,* p. 30.
[31] Beck, *op. cit.,* p. 125.

that such power so used was a threat to the integrity of boards of control of state universities.[32]

Information on the removal of board members obtained for 87 boards of state controlled institutions documents the power of the state executive office. Just as the governor of the state is the primary individual involved in appointment of trustees to these institutional boards, so is he the key person in action for their removal. Either alone, or jointly with the legislature or board, the governor can remove members in over half of the 187 boards studied. Other procedures for removal of board members included court proceedings, action of the board itself, and independent action of the legislature. Only four of the boards reported no established machinery for removal of board members. As a general rule, removal may be only for "cause." [33]

Ideally, the conditions of tenure should guarantee that turnover of members will not be so rapid as to cause instability but rapid enough to prevent crystallization of viewpoint or background among the members. How to maintain a proper balance between these two undesirable extremes is a question that has long plagued scholars in college administration. Over a half-century ago, Charles W. Eliot advised boards of trustees to resist the natural tendency ". . . to fill a vacancy by electing some contemporary of the remaining members . . ." but to assure a fresh viewpoint on the board by filling ". . . each successive vacancy in the board from a generation younger than that to which most of the surviving members belong. . . ." [34]

Present practices of establishing overlapping terms of office of at least six years' duration and protecting members from capricious dismissal suggest success in keeping turnover from becoming too high. No similar evidence supports clearly a conclusion that the related objective of assuring a desirable minimum degree of turnover is being met. Perhaps a limited claim for such a conclusion, at least for publicly supported institutions, can be justified on the basis that Chambers in 1937 reported an average term of actual service on the boards of state universities to be twelve years, whereas the comparable finding from the study of state boards made some twenty

---

[32] M. M. Chambers, "Tenure of State University Trustees," *Educational Record,* XVIII (January, 1937), 125-36.

[33] Martorana and Hollis, *op. cit.,* pp. 29-30.

[34] Charles W. Eliot, *University Administration* (Boston: Houghton Mifflin Company, 1908), p. 4.

years later, was seven years.[35] To this writer's knowledge, even such tenuous evidence is lacking for a similar conclusion about boards of privately controlled institutions.

Size of Boards

Board size has direct bearing on two important issues in the administration of higher education. One is representative of the institution served and understanding of institutional operation. The second is administrative manageability—that is, ease of communication among members, attainment of reasonably high attendance at meetings, and orderliness of conduct and discussion at board meetings. Stress upon the first issue leads to a conclusion that to be effective a board should be quite large; emphasis of the second suggests that the number of members should be rather limited. In practice a balance between the advantages of large and small boards has to be achieved.

Range in size of boards. Actually, the range in number of members on the approximately 1000 boards responsible for higher institutions is astonishing. Some have as few as three members while others have more than a hundred. The range extends to both publicly and privately controlled baccalaureate institutions. Two studies of boards of publicly controlled institutions, using different sources of data, report an average number of between ten and eleven members.[36] Both of these studies considered only the size of boards of publicly controlled institutions granting baccalaureate degrees. If they had also included the membership of boards which governed the more than three hundred local public two-year colleges, the average figure would have been much lower because two-year college boards are generally smaller. A tabulation of the institutional exhibits in *American Junior Colleges, 1960,* completed by this writer showed the publicly supported two-year colleges boards range in size from three to thirty, with a median of seven members.

Membership data of governing, governing-coordinating, coordinating, and "other" boards showed the same average membership for governing-coordinating boards as for the total 209 boards in the 1959 study cited above: 10.6. To arrive at this average membership

---

[35] Chambers, *op. cit.,* p. 125; and Martorana and Hollis, *op. cit.,* p. 30.
[36] Eells, *op. cit.,* p. 340; and Martorana and Hollis, *op. cit.,* p. 28.

for governing-coordinating boards and in order to present a truer picture, the 102-member Board of Trustees of the University of North Carolina was excluded. The membership of the remaining governing-coordinating boards ranged from a low of four to a high of 32. The average membership for coordinating boards was slightly higher—twelve in nearest round numbers—and that for governing and "other" boards slightly lower—rounding out to ten members. The range of membership found for these three types of public boards was: coordinating, 9–18, governing, 3–32; and "other" 3–21.[37]

Among privately controlled institutions the range in board size is about the same as for public colleges, as has been noted, but the median, except for institutions related to the Roman Catholic Church, is much larger. Eells reports for privately controlled baccalaureate institutions median numbers of board members as follows: independent institutions, 23; Protestant denominations, 30; Roman Catholic, 7; and for all privately controlled institutions, 24.[38] The tabulation made by the author of the privately controlled junior colleges showed a range of from 3–60, and a median which rounded out to 17 members.

Effect of size on board operations.   The overall tendency of board size centering around ten members in the publicly controlled institutions reflects recognition of three possible factors: (1) a larger group can become unwieldy, with the possibility of factions developing among the members; (2) conflicts of dates for meetings are more probable in a larger group; and (3) travel and per diem costs present problems when boards are very large. On the other hand, founders of privately controlled institutions may favor larger boards because of (1) the broad geographic dispersal of the constituency of the institution, (2) the need to recruit students on a large geographic base, and (3) the need to obtain contributions to finance the institution's operations and construction costs.

Statements to support both boards with large and with relatively small memberships are to be found in the writings on college administration. But clearcut definition of what is a "large" or a "small" board is lacking. One encounters the statement, for example, that "Because of historical circumstances the Board of Higher Education

---

[37] Martorana and Hollis, *op. cit.,* pp. 28-29.
[38] Eells, *op. cit.,* p. 340.

is of unwieldy size with 22 members. For this reason its work is done mainly in committee." [39] Yet a board of such size or even larger is supported by E. H. Dana because it contributes to broader representation of the institution's constituency and to acquisition of needed financial resources.[40] After discussing some weaknesses that he had observed in boards of trustees, Cummings recommended that the most common flagrant shortcomings could be reduced by minimizing the size of the board.[41] And Ruml and Morrison advise substitution of membership or addition of persons on the board when it does not include ". . . sufficient members presently able to discharge adequately their responsibilities as Trustees of their college." [42]

Such statements mainly reiterate the advantages and disadvantages set forth by proponents of large or small boards almost three decades ago.[43] As yet, however, the vital question of how and when a board can be declared inadequate to serve its functions because of size has not been objectively determined. This lack of objectively ascertainable relationship led Russell and Reeves to exclude the factor of size from those considered in the accrediting process set forth in the early 1930's.[44] Logic and subjective evaluations, however, suggest that size does bear meaningfully on board operations and therefore on the development of institutional excellence. Where very large or unusually small boards control institutions of recognized excellence, it may be suspected that some compensating administrative arrangements have emerged to offset the weaknesses of size. These may result either by deliberate action or unobtrusively as the board works out its *modus operandi*.

Techniques of achieving effectiveness in boards of varying sizes. The usual outcome of efforts to compensate for extreme board size, large or small, is a pattern of board organization which places a

---

[39] Freda R. H. Martens, "The City University of New York—Its Origin and Present Status." Unpublished mimeographed paper presented to the Board of Higher Education, New York, June 27, 1961.

[40] E. H. Dana, "Why College Trustees?" *Journal of Higher Education*, XVIII (May, 1947), 259-62.

[41] E. C. Cummings, "Some Observations on the Trustees," *School and Society*, LXXVII (January 3, 1953), 1-3.

[42] Beardsley Ruml and Donald H. Morrison, *Memo to a College Trustee: A Report of the Financial and Structural Problems of the Liberal College* (New York: McGraw-Hill Book Company, 1959), p. 77.

[43] Elliott, Chambers, and Ashbrook, *op. cit.*, pp. 31-32.

[44] Russell and Reeves, *op. cit.*, 29.

heavy responsibility on a small central body or executive committee, but involves a much larger group. Where the board of trustees is officially required to be large, the total membership must, of course, vote on matters for the formal record. The usual practice in voting, however, is to follow the recommendation of subcommittees of the board and the executive committee. A similar pattern is often found where the board is small. Here the board's reach is extended by fact-finding bodies used in an advisory capacity, and the official board assumes a role of reviewing body and final deciding agency.

It is difficult to relate always the development of such a pattern to the initial size of the official board, for in some instances the pattern has been set forth in the initial documents of the institution. Whether or not this is true, however, the intent is to extend the reach of the board while placing most—if not all—of the general management of the institution in the smaller group.

Among the institutions which have an officially established bi-cameral board are Harvard and Western Reserve. In its charter of 1650, Harvard designated for its central government ". . . a Corporation consisting of seven persons (to wit) a President, five Fellows, and a Treasurer or Bursar. . . ." Although this charter makes mention of the "Overseers" and indicates that their concurrence must be obtained on several important matters, it does not stipulate the membership and duties of the Overseers in the precise and complete fashion that those of the Corporation are set forth.[45] The present government of the University includes 32 Overseers, two selected *ex officio,* and thirty elected by the alumni for six-year terms.

Western Reserve University adopted a similar board structure in more recent times. This University has a Board of Trustees of fifteen members of which twelve are elected by the Board of Governors for six-year terms, and three, including the president of the institution and the chairman of the Board of Governors, are *ex officio* members. The Board of Governors consists of 60 members, including one alumnus from each division of the university, civic leaders, and three *ex officio* members. That this structure was intended to expand the outlook of the board is reported by President John Millis who

---

[45] Richard Hofstadter and Wilson Smith, eds., *American Higher Education, A Documentary History,* Volume I (Chicago: The University of Chicago Press, 1961), pp. 10-12.

headed the university at the time the new organizational structure for the trustees was established.[46]

Many illustrations could be given of large boards of trustees which have organized into an executive committee and other standing or working committees in order to expedite the functioning of the board. Reference has been made above to the Board of Higher Education in New York City. Others will be discussed in the section on board organization and conduct of board business in the next chapter. Advisory agencies are used extensively by boards related to the Roman Catholic Church and those which control local public junior colleges. Both groups of institutions have relatively small boards. The purposes for establishing advisory boards in the first group of institutions appear in the following statement:

> In fact, it serves a very useful purpose (1) in keeping the institution in touch with social trends and needs; (2) in providing stimulating extra-institutional viewpoints and standards; (3) in securing and offering financial help and advice; (4) in helping with the promotion and conduct of drives for funds; (5) in establishing and fostering good public relations; (6) in giving advice on legal problems; (7) in referring conflicts with pressure groups; (8) in representing the institution according to instructions before legislative bodies.[47]

With the possible exception of the statement referring to drives for funds, these functions are also commonly set forth for advisory bodies to boards of publicly controlled institutions.

Other Characteristics of Boards of Trustees

Several other aspects of the composition of boards responsible for higher institutions could have been presented in this chapter. Little or nothing has been said, for example, about residence requirements of trustees, the extent to which boards have among their members persons on the salaried staff of the institutions controlled, or pay for trustees for their services. These were not amplified because of limitations of space as well as because of the belief that they were not as

---

[46] Personal interview with President John S. Millis, Western Reserve University in Chicago, Ill., March 4, 1961.

[47] Alcuin W. Tasch, *op. cit.,* p. 67.

critical as those factors that were discussed. It should be noted, however, that residence specifications do not necessarily guarantee broader representativeness of the board. Nevertheless, such stipulations are to be found—especially among publicly controlled state-supported institutions.[48] Historically, it has been considered poor administrative practice to include employed staff members on boards which set general policy. Growing questioning of this principle appears in more recent writings, and greater attention to this subject therefore is given in Chapter V. On the matter of compensation for board members, however, the historical authoritative position that membership on boards responsible for higher education is a social service persists. Except for reimbursement for expenses incurred on board business, financial payment is generally frowned upon.

It is essential that boards be composed of men and women of character, demonstrated capacity, and strong interest in public service. These considerations should govern appointments, not such specific characteristics as occupation, race, sex, religion, or education.

---

[48] Martorana and Hollis, *op. cit.*, p. 30.

CHAPTER IV

Board Operations and the Administrative Process

The ultimate test of the effectiveness of a board of trustees is the results that come from participation in the administrative process. If the board's participation in this process is effective, it will contribute to stability of institutional operation, sound changes as conditions change, and demonstrable accomplishments of institutional objectives. When administrative strength and leadership are lacking in the board, negative effects can usually be expected.

Among the different types of boards responsible for higher institutions (see Chapter II), those classified as governing or as governing and coordinating boards are active participants in all aspects of administration. Only these kinds of boards are considered in this chapter, which deals with the role of the board of trustees in administration. Decision to exclude coordinating boards from the discussion stemmed from two reasons: first, they act only through other boards which govern the institutions, and, second, limitations of space precluded adequate discussion of the effect these coordinating or "super" boards have on governing boards in the administrative process.

Obligations to Legal Authority and Responsibility

The duties and powers that are legally imposed on boards of trustees of colleges and universities are a definite mandate to participate in the administration of institutional affairs. Indeed, the language of state constitutions and statutes pertaining to publicly controlled institutions and that of charters granted to privately controlled colleges usually very clearly indicates that, in the legal sense, the board of trustees *is* the institution. Thus, for example, the legal basis for the operation of the University of California is found in the statement:

The University of California shall constitute a public trust, to be administered by the existing corporation as "The Regents of the University of California," with full powers of organization and government, subject only to such legislative control as may be necessary to insure compliance with the terms of the endowments of the University and the security of its funds.[1]

In the original documents relating to Stanford University appear such statements concerning the powers and duties of the board of trustees as "To manage and control the institution hereby founded," "To make By-laws not inconsistent with the laws of this State, or the purposes of this grant, for the government of the Institution hereby founded," and "To fix the salaries of the President, professors, and teachers and to fix them at such rates as will secure the University the services of men of the very highest attainment." [2]

The language of the founding documents of institutions and boards to control them differs from one to another, and the degree of authority—especially with respect to publicly controlled institutions—varies from state to state. The generalization that boards of trustees have very large powers over their institutions, however, is strong and inescapable.

With this comprehensive official authority and responsibility, it is evident that boards could rule over their institutions in an entirely autocratic manner. Some writers have concluded that as a general rule this is the case. Beck states: "Almost without exception in this country, governing boards exercise these powers and functions without the consent of the governed . . ." [3] and Capen depicts university administration as a "simon pure example of authoritarian government." [4]

Others, however, have found that the inherent character of the academic community precludes a drastic board authoritarianism in the administrative process. Corson advances the thesis that an institution of higher learning is a government in itself and therefore has characteristics in common with other social and civic groups. He

---

[1] The Constitution of the State of California, as amended November 5, 1918. Sec. 9, Article IX.

[2] "The Founding Grant of November 11, 1885," *Administrative Manual for Trustees, Officers, and Faculty of The Leland Stanford Junior University* (Stanford, Calif.: Stanford University, 1959), pp. 1-5.

[3] Beck, *Men Who Control Our Universities, op. cit.,* p. 30.

[4] Capen, *The Management of Universities* (Buffalo, N.Y.: Foster and Stewart Publishing Corporation, 1953), p. 7.

goes on, however, to point out three significant differences from other forms of enterprise:

> 1. Colleges and, to a still greater degree, universities exist to serve a multiplicity of purposes. . . . 2. The college, and to a lesser degree the university, is more dispersed as an enterprise than the typical business enterprise or governmental agency. . . . 3. The responsibility for making decisions is more widely diffused.[5]

In actual practice, therefore, boards of trustees delegate much of their authority to other segments of the academic community. They thereby assume a different position in the administrative process. The position of the board in best practice is one in which broad matters of policy are reviewed and acted upon at the board level, leaving through delegated authority the subordinate points of policy and the day-to-day executive and management functions to the administrative staff and the faculty.

Delegation rights and procedures. Many factors make delegation of board authority a practical necessity. Besides the unique characteristics of a higher institution as described by Corson above, there is the fact that board members are busy persons in their own spheres of business and civic affairs. Their time for personal participation in administering institutional affairs is limited. Moreover, as persons usually without specific training in higher education—a highly specialized or technical endeavor, board members generally need to rely on professional staff members for executive implementation of their policies.

Administrative efficiency, then, is the primary justification for delegation by the board of authority to other components in the administrative structure. The board, however, retains ultimate responsibility, as Blackwell clearly states:

> In this country, the governing board of a non-public college or university has plenary authority, limited only by the provision of its charter, the laws of the land, and public opinion. Much of this authority is usually delegated to the president, the chief executive officer of the institution. The president, in turn, delegates many of his duties and responsibilities to his administrative officers, deans and faculty committees. However, the governing board remains the

---

[5] John J. Corson, *Governance of Colleges and Universities* (New York: McGraw-Hill Book Company, Inc., 1960), pp. 9-10.

repository of power since it may, at its pleasure, withhold or withdraw its delegation of power.[6]

Delegation of board authority is usually of two types: delegation to committees of the board, either standing or *ad hoc,* or delegation to individuals—most often the president of the institution, the chief executive officer of the board. Use of both types of delegation and their joint relationship to the board and institutional effectiveness has long been recognized. Russell and Reeves advanced consideration of this function in the accreditation of higher institutions, stating:

> There has been a rather universally accepted opinion among educators that the functions of the board of control and of committees of the board should be the consideration and approval of policies rather than the execution of these policies. The board may properly act either directly or through its committees on any question in which its legal responsibilities are involved (for example, court actions or the signing of contracts) or on matters affecting the administration of invested funds. On other matters the board is expected to act through its constituted executive officers. This principle does not preclude action of an advisory nature by the board or by committees of the board, but there should be no interference by the board with the detailed administration of the institution. It has further been suggested that the board should act either as a whole or through committees with specifically delegated power; it should be clear that the members of the board have no power individually to make decisions concerning the institution except as that power has been specifically delegated to them by the board itself.[7]

Since the most common individual delegation of board authority is to the president, who is responsible for institutional management, there develops in colleges a hierarchy or scalar pattern of administrative levels akin to that found in the structure for administration of other enterprises. Scholars of academic administration, however, repeatedly stress that the scalar concept of administration has only limited application in this field. Corson states:

---

[6] Thomas E. Blackwell, *College Law: A Guide for Administrators* (Washington, D.C.: The American Council on Education, 1951), p. 40.

[7] John Dale Russell and Floyd W. Reeves, *The Evaluation of Higher Institutions,* Vol. VI: *Administration* (Chicago: The University of Chicago Press, 1936), p. 27.

... to understand the governance of colleges and universities requires the recognition of the fact that the *scalar principle,* so firmly imbedded in the minds of those acquainted with business, governmental, and military organizations, has no duplicate in the academic enterprise. The roles of the trustees, the presidents, the deans, the department head, and the faculty (or faculties) have a surface similarity to the scalar organization found in other enterprises, but a basic dissimilarity.[8]

Various writers have attempted to describe the unique character of a college which makes full application of a highly structured administrative hierarchy impractical. Logan Wilson, on the basis of an analysis of the social structure of university professional staffs, attributed one factor to be the large number of staff members who possess high professional competence. Such professional personnel, when working outside the academic setting, are generally private practitioners and self-employed. He draws the conclusion that: "Between the individualistic and hierarchal poles, the social organization of the university occupies a rather anomalous position." [9] On this point, Ruml and Morrison appear to agree when they observe: "The 'chain of command' in a college is at most a tenuous line of influence. The President and deans must rely primarily upon departmental chairmen to direct and influence the departments." [10]

How much of the board's authority should be delegated to committees of the board and to the president and through him to lower echelon administrative staff members and the faculty is a delicate administrative question. The general rule, drawn from authoritative writings on the subject, is that the board should retain the responsibility to decide—with the assistance of recommendations advanced by employed staff and others—the main policies within which the institution will operate. Thus the board charts the course of development and molds overall institutional character. Within this general framework, executive actions and power to make subordinate decisions are delegated to the officers of administration and faculty.

In practical operations the board itself answers the question of

---

[8] Corson, *op. cit.,* p. 15.

[9] Logan Wilson, *The Academic Man* (New York: Oxford University Press, 1942), p. 72.

[10] Beardsley Ruml and Donald H. Morrison, *Memo to a College Trustee* (New York: McGraw-Hill Book Company, 1959), p. 56.

the degree of delegation to be allowed, though many pressures and factors bear on the decision. Underdelegation of board authority, leads to board autocracy and conditions that support the view that there is control "without the consent of the governed." Overdelegation, on the other hand, leads to a confusion of institutional purpose and misunderstanding as to where the responsibility for policy determination and executive decision truly lies.

Experienced administrators as well as scholars in higher education disagree on the extent to which board authority can be appropriately delegated. A common view is also lacking on the proper locus of responsibility for direction of various phases of institutional affairs. Cowley, for example, makes clear his position that while faculties can cooperate in academic government if they so desire, they cannot seek realistically to control it. He says: "Observe that I say *participation in academic government* and not *control* of it. Some professors continue to advocate the adoption of the historic French system of academic government. . . . Our whole legal structure stands in the way. . . ." [11]

An almost opposite position is suggested by Hughes when he describes the relative roles of the trustees, president, and faculty:

> The trustees control all financial and property matters and determine general policies. The president administers the institution under policies fixed by the trustees. The faculty controls teaching and research and is responsible for academic standards. [12]

A rationale that supports the stand represented in Hughes' statement has been advanced by Penrose at the conclusion of a comparative study of the structure of higher education in the United States and in the Netherlands:

> Accomplishing the objectives of the institution depends on the willingness of competent people to engage in the kind of behavior which taken together will further institutional purposes. Thus in a real sense, it is the professor who gives authority to the adminis-

---

[11] W. H. Cowley, "The Administration of American Colleges and Universities," in Oswald Nielsen, ed., *University Administration in Practice* (Stanford, Calif.: Stanford University Graduate School of Business, 1959), p. 9.

[12] Raymond M. Hughes, *A Manual for Trustees of Colleges and Universities* (Ames, Iowa: The Iowa State College Press, 1943), p. 11.

trator, not the board of trustees. Authority and responsibility are delegated "up" the hierarchy, not down.[13]

This view is debatable, as the statements from Blackwell, Chambers, and Cowley above indicate. At any rate, its presence and the firmness of conviction of those who hold it show that trustees need to recognize the faculty in making decisions concerning institutional affairs, particularly in the realms of curriculum and instruction.

Wisdom in the exercise of trusteeship requires constant surveillance to protect the advantages of democratic administration. Within this process, however, the authority of the board and its responsibility remain, and in the last analysis the board must look after the control of the institution.

Control rights and procedures. In any enterprise involving the control of people, effectiveness of control is related to the controlling agency's closeness to those who are controlled. Boards of trustees, as controlling agencies, need therefore to maintain a constant and close understanding of institutional matters and to use techniques of control which contribute to mutual understanding and respect among board, administration, and faculty. The Dimocks, in their volume, *Public Administration,* make a distinction between two concepts of control: executive or administrative and democratic control. They state that the democratic principle requires exercise of control over policy or action to be placed as close to the people controlled as is feasibly possible, all other principles taken into account.[14]

Both types of control are found in well-managed higher institutions. Executive or administrative control is evident in the use of regular and official reporting procedures throughout the administrative structure of the institutions. Boards of trustees see the culmination of these procedures in the reports and proposals for action made to them by their chief executive officers. Major reports of this kind include the annual report of the president on the general management of institutional affairs and the annual presentation of the budget for operations and for capital outlay. Such devices as letters

13 William O. Penrose, *Structure of Higher Education.* Institute of Social Studies Publication on Social Change, No. 17, Netherlands Universities Foundation for International Cooperation. (The Hague, Netherlands: Van Keulen Publishers, 1960), p. 179.

14 M. E. Dimock and G. O. Dimock, *Public Administration* (New York: Holt, Rinehart & Winston, 1953), p. 86.

or memos to the board, reports on topics of special study or action, and materials to accompany the agenda of meetings are other means whereby the board of trustees keeps close to the institution. Actions taken on proposals which pass through these procedures represent the board's control of the institution.

Closeness of control on institutional matters and operations varies widely. Sometimes a very close control is required by laws or by the charter of the college or colleges concerned. A member of the Regents of South Dakota, for example, must act on all requisitions for expenditures, a given Regent each year serving for each college in the state system as its "institutional committee" for this and other purposes.[15] Such closeness of control, however, is the exception rather than the rule in the administration of American higher education.

Relations with other agencies. Maintaining the operations for a college or university is a complex enterprise both in academic matters and in supporting business affairs. The undertaking rests on a matrix of contracts of many kinds. In these the rights and duties of the board to acquire and dispose of property, to handle funds, to purchase materials, to commit the institution to personnel policies, and many other areas of activity become real—not mere theoretical considerations. Relationships which result between boards of trustees and other agencies may be grouped into two broad categories: governmental, including state, local, and federal agencies of government; and nongovernmental, covering a host of organizations and associations. Generally speaking, publicly controlled higher institutions have more dealings with governmental agencies than those that are privately controlled, but this is by no means a small matter even among the latter type of institutions.

Dealings with local and state agencies which have particular legal functions to perform are often encountered in the conduct of official business of the board of trustees. At the local level, for example, these may include city planning commissions that are concerned with land use and zoning regulations; local law enforcement agencies concerned with the control of traffic, personal safety of citizens,

---

[15] S. V. Martorana, Ernest V. Hollis, and Staff Members of the Division of Higher Education, *Higher Education in South Dakota: A Report of a Survey* (Pierre, S.D.: Legislative Research Council, 1960), p. 34.

and safeguarding of property; public utility commissions; local boards of education; and many others.

Some of the state agencies that are frequently involved are the state education department, the attorney general, special building authorities or commissions, civil service commissions, and purchasing and auditing agencies. Privately controlled institutions, although generally more free of these associations than the public colleges and universities, are not completely so in all states. To cite one example, any privately controlled higher institution wishing to offer a new degree in New York State must first acquire the approval of the Regents of the University of the State of New York.

Within recent years the involvement of higher institutions in programs of the federal government has shown steady increase. Several thorough analyses of the impact of these programs on the colleges and universities have been made—the general inquiry being directed, however, to the relationships between the governmental programs and the program of instruction and the staff of the institution rather than toward the obligations and role of the boards of trustees.[16] Trustees of both publicly and privately controlled institutions, however, need to understand the advantages and disadvantages of institutional participation in such governmental programs and the necessity of clear policy lines to guide and direct the participation. That governmental programs are influencing heavily the boards of privately controlled institutions is indicated in the following statement made at a national gathering of church-related colleges:

> This movement into certain techniques of meeting the financial obligations of a long-range plan raises another question that must be met practically as well as philosophically. Do we as church-related colleges wish to use government funds to help realize certain aspects of our long-range plans? This question must be faced whether we find it distasteful or not since the government has been, and is, directly involved in education.[17]

---

[16] See for example: Homer D. Babbidge, Jr. and Robert M. Rosenzweig, *The Federal Interest in Higher Education* (New York: McGraw-Hill Book Company, 1962); Charles V. Kidd, *American Universities and Federal Research* (Cambridge, Mass.: Harvard University Press, 1959); and J. Kenneth Little, "Federal Programs in a State University," *Higher Education*, XVII (October, 1960), 3-6.

[17] Woodrow A. Geier, *Effective Trustees: A Report,* National Conference of Trustees for Church Colleges at Lake Junaluska, North Carolina, June 26-28, 1959 (Nashville, Tenn.: Division of Educational Institutions, Board of Education, The Methodist Church, 1959), p. 90.

The courts are another type of governmental agency with which higher institutions are often involved, a fact well-documented in the classic work by M. M. Chambers.[18] Use of the courts in resolving complicated issues and clarifying vague points of board authority and jurisdiction can be of substantial aid to a board of trustees. The courts, therefore, should be viewed by boards as resources by which —if need arises—board prerogatives can be emphasized and protected and the erosion of board authority by actions of other agencies or by legislation conflicting with constitutional or statutory authority of the board prevented.

Boards of trustees must also discharge their legal obligation in dealing with nongovernmental agencies. The array of these defies listing for it would include the regional accrediting associations, such as the North Central Association of Colleges and Secondary Schools; professional associations, such as the American Medical Association, which also accredit particular academic programs; labor unions with which members of the nonacademic staff may be affiliated; the American Association of University Professors and other professional associations to which members of the faculty belong; boards of trustees of hospitals, libraries, museums, or other such institutions; boards of trustees of other colleges and universities with which formal cooperative interinstitutional ventures might be undertaken; and many others. Wherever relationships with these agencies bear on institutions for which they are responsible, boards of trustees must act. In this action, board attention should concentrate on matters that are truly of a policy nature and not executive action. Each board member can help his institution best by recognizing and adhering to this basic principle.

Board Organization and Conduct of Business

In view of the position of critical importance that boards of trustees hold in higher education, the paucity of research and scholarly writing pertaining to the organization and methods of operation of these bodies is striking. Eells and Hollis, in their extensive bibliography of writings on the administration of higher education, list

---

[18] Merritt M. Chambers, *The Colleges and the Courts: Decisions Regarding Higher Education in the United States,* 3 Volumes (New York: Carnegie Corporation, 1941, 1946, and 1952).

thirty-five references which deal with boards of control. Fewer than a half dozen of these deal with the internal organization of the boards and their business procedures.[19] Lack of attention to this matter may have been a contributing reason why the Association of Governing Boards organized a "School for Regents" in which much discussion was given to board organization and procedures for operation.[20]

Board officers and their duties.   Based upon reports given by representatives of some fifty boards of control of state universities and colleges at the School for Regents, the most commonly found officers of boards of trustees are the chairman and secretary, though in some cases a vice-chairman and treasurer are also named.[21] These officials are usually selected by the board members themselves but there are some interesting departures from this general rule. The chairman and vice-chairman of the board of trustees of the State University of New York, for example, are designated by the governor.

In some instances (see Chapter III), the president of the college may also be a member of the board of trustees. This creates a point of confusion in the administrative structure. Among the privately controlled institutions especially, the distinction between the officers of the board and the officers of the institution is often not clear. In this connection, Elliott, Chambers, and Ashbrook advance a strong recommendation for improvement of board bylaws by the inclusion of clear statements distinguishing the duties of officers of the board, elected from its membership, as opposed to the responsibilities of its employed professional staff, particularly the president of the institution.[22]

The duties of the chairman of the board are those usual to the

---

[19] Walter Crosby Eells and Ernest V. Hollis, *Administration of Higher Education: An Annotated Bibliography,* Office of Education Circular OE-53002, 1960, No. 7 (Washington, D.C.: USGPO, 1960), pp. 113-18.

[20] "School for Regents," *Proceedings,* Association of Governing Boards of State Universities and Allied Institutions. 39th Annual Meeting, Lincoln, Nebraska, October 10-14, 1961 (Denver, Colo.: Association of Governing Boards, 1962), pp. 25-34.

[21] From notes taken personally by author at the School for Regents, Lincoln, Nebraska, October 10-14, 1961.

[22] Edward C. Elliott, M. M. Chambers, and William A. Ashbrook, *The Government of Higher Education* (New York: American Book Company, 1935), p. 112.

head of an organization. He presides at meetings, signs legal and official documents recording actions of the board as a body corporate, and generally gives leadership to the board in carrying out its prescribed duties. In this position he clearly is a key figure in the board's overall effectiveness. He can help develop coherence and unanimity of purpose while encouraging and protecting a healthy difference of opinion among members of the board. He can assure board understanding of the institution by the kind and extent of informational material he requests from the president and supporting professional staff. And he can keep the board members' attention and energy oriented constantly to matters of high policy rather than executive or administrative details.

The secretary of the board has the obligation of keeping the official seal of the board and maintaining the records of board meetings and other official actions. This is an important function that is needed not only for legal purposes, but also for such advantages as facilitating the orientation and induction of new board members, assuring the orderly and evolutionary development of new policies as conditions change, and promoting systematic communication of board actions to faculty, alumni, and other interested groups.

The secretary of the board also frequently carries responsibility for board correspondence, compiles the agenda of meetings, and distributes the minutes of meetings and related reports. Because these duties are closely related to the work of the president of the institution as chief executive officer of the board, it is not unusual to see this official designated by law, charter, or board bylaws as having the function also of secretary of the board.

Although research evidence is lacking on the subject, there appears to this writer to be a tendency away from the employment of persons outside the professional staff of the institution to serve as secretary or as treasurer of the board. The preferred practice is for the president of the institution to serve also as secretary of the board, with supporting staff to help in the routine duties of the assignment. This statement is supported by the facts reported and the subsequent group discussion on administrative responsibility of boards recorded at the 1961 School for Regents mentioned above. The concept is also suggested in Dodds' recommendation that an "assistant to the president" have duties that are combined with those of the secretary of the board because the two functions form a "natural unit." [23] The observation is also consistent with the answer given by Elliott, Chambers, and Ashbrook to the question of which officers of the board should be selected from its own membership:

> Only the chairman and the vice-chairman should be elected by the board from its own membership. . . . The work of taking minutes of the board and preserving its records, of notifying trustees of meetings, and of affixing the seal of the institution should be delegated to a staff officer who is responsible to the president of the institution.[24]

The length of term of board officers bears directly on the stability of the board and the balance desired between stability and helpful change of viewpoint, and in methods of conducting board affairs that come from changes in the leadership positions. Perusal of the reference volumes on colleges and universities published by the American Council on Education and other published writings on college administration reveals that the great majority of boards elect their officers annually. This does not establish, however, the total tenure of a given slate of officers. It is a well-known fact that in some institutions the same person is elected chairman of the board year after year. This places a great dependence for leadership on the personality of one individual. Although in some cases it may produce excellent results, the practice as a general rule is discouraged.

Board committees. Use of standing committees by boards of trustees varies greatly. This is apparent both from the reports of representatives who attended the School for Trustees at Lincoln, Nebraska and from the writings on this subject. Where the size of the board membership and the ability of members to attend meetings allow, the preferred practice is for the board of trustees to act as a "committee of the whole" on all except strictly temporary matters. To handle tasks that fall into the latter grouping, *ad hoc* and fact-finding committees are usually established to give the board a sounder basis for action.

When practical circumstances prohibit the functioning of the board as a single body, the general practice is to establish an executive committee of the board. This group then acts for the board

---

[23] Harold W. Dodds, *The Academic President—Educator or Caretaker* (New York: McGraw-Hill Book Company, 1962), p. 94.

[24] Elliott, Chambers, and Ashbrook, *op. cit.,* pp. 117-18.

between meetings and carries on its work in close association with the president and administrative staff of the institution. Chapter II, in the section dealing with size of boards, noted some institutions which have in effect a bicameral board with one part carrying out certain noncontrolling functions and another designated more particularly for governing purposes. The usual standing committees, besides the executive committee, are those which deal with investments, budgetary matters, and physical facilities. These were found to be the common committees among the boards of fifteen institutions of higher learning studied recently by Corson.[25] Hughes mentions these and adds another committee dealing with "education and faculty." He concludes his analysis with the observation: "An inspection of catalogues discloses a great variety of other committees determined by the needs of the several institutions." [26]

One type of committee found frequently in use by governing-coordinating boards is that which functions as a subgoverning board responsible for one of the institutions in the overall system. Such a system has existed for many years, for example, in South Dakota. Use of such subgoverning boards, when the board at the higher level also has governing and controlling powers, is considered poor administrative practice and abandonment of the system has been recommended for South Dakota and elsewhere.[27]

Boards of trustees should be judicious in the use of both standing and *ad hoc* committees. Neither type should cause neglect of the basic principle that the board is a body corporate and that its basic worth as well as its responsibility to the institution governed lies in its collective wisdom and actions. In the words of Ruml and Morrison:

> The existence of standing committees helps in dividing the word of Trustees, but the standing committee can be improperly used to conceal as well as to inform. The ad-hoc Special Committee is likely to serve a useful purpose if the members will cooperate and not leave the chairman with an issue too hot to handle in an open Board meeting.[28]

Board meetings. Practice of boards of trustees on the number and types of meetings held seems to vary considerably between those

---

[25] Corson, *op. cit.*, p. 51.
[26] Hughes, *op. cit.*, p. 8.
[27] Martorana, Hollis, *et al.*, *op. cit.*, Vol. I, p. 37.
[28] Ruml and Morrison, *op. cit.*, p. 78.

responsible for publicly supported institutions and those responsible for privately controlled institutions. Meetings of boards of publicly controlled higher learning are generally open to the public. About 85 per cent of the 134 boards responsible for public institutions studied by this writer and Hollis reported that their meetings were open to the public.[29] Though a comparable study of boards of privately controlled colleges is lacking, the general observation is that these do not hold open meetings.

Boards of publicly controlled institutions also meet more often than those responsible for privately controlled colleges and universities. This may be due to several factors such as: (1) the members, coming all from one state as opposed to the more geographically widespread residence of trustees of private institutions, can attend meetings more conveniently; (2) the smaller memberships of public boards as opposed to private ones; and (3) the fact that boards of trustees of public institutions are in many instances required by law to hold a specified number of meetings each year. The study cited above found that all but two of the 150 state boards for which these data were available had a legal minimum number of meetings to be held each year, the average requirement being four meetings annually. In actual practice, however, the boards were found to meet on an average of nine times a year, over two times the average number required. In contrast the fifteen institutional boards that Corson studied, all but three of which controlled privately controlled higher institutions, met four to six times a year.[30]

Both the number and the types of meetings held raise some basic questions about the effectiveness of practice among boards of trustees. The number and complexity of the problems which must be dealt with in the direction of higher institutions would indicate that meetings could be held to advantage at least nine times a year and that a greater flexibility in types of meetings would be desirable. As a matter of fact, the holding of "special" meetings in addition to "regular" meetings is common practice when board attention must be directed to unusual or pressing problems. Contrary to the usual practice for "regular" meetings, "special" meetings of public boards are usually closed sessions. Besides holding both "regular" and "spe-

---

[29] Martorana and Hollis, *State Boards Responsible for Higher Education, op. cit.,* p. 33.
[30] Corson, *op. cit.,* p. 50.

cial" meetings, some boards hold briefing sessions—for board members and members of the administrative staff of the institution in advance of the official meeting.

In the absence of enough meetings to assure full board attention to basic institutional policy development, there usually develops one of two patterns. Either the president, his staff, and the faculty of the institution assume both policy and executive functions; or committees of the board take over the overall board role. Corson's study found that the latter development is commonplace and reports his findings as follows:

> Meetings, therefore, tend to be formal affairs for official approval of matters previously worked out by the president, the board chairman, and committees. As a rule, significant decision making does not occur at official board meetings, particularly by the larger boards.[31]

Recording and reporting decisions. For many reasons, boards of trustees need to establish sound practices and policies for recording and reporting their decisions. Most fundamental perhaps is that there must be a record that can be used with confidence whenever legal and financial questions are raised. A well-kept system of board records, however, is useful also in the orientation of new board members, the induction of presidents and other staff members, studies for the evaluation of board and institutional operations, and related purposes.

The official record of board actions appears in the minutes of board meetings and in documents concerning legal and business transactions of the institution. The former generally records the subjects of board attention, reports of fact-finding efforts by board committees or the administrative staff, the tenor of discussion, and official actions. Actual minutes vary greatly in content, some giving a complete summary of the foregoing points and others giving only the barest of information on formal actions taken. A well-kept and thorough record ideally should allow relationships to be drawn between policies set by the board for institutional operation and development and subsequent official executive or operating actions. Thus, it would be possible to find in the board minutes a record of the discussion and establishment of a policy and later in time to find

---

[31] *Ibid.*, p. 51.

in the documents of institutional operations evidence of implementation of the policy.

Simply recording board actions, decisions, and policies is not sufficient to assure good administration. There must also be a complete and continuing program of communication whereby the policies of the board are made known and kept current among administrative staff members, the faculties, and the constituency served. Bad communications, as Monro points out, often lead to misunderstanding and academic and administrative troubles.[32] He and Mather report, moreover, that deficiency in communications contributes to confusion of function between the administrative and academic elements in higher institutions; both use as illustration the ambiguities that exist in many institutions with respect to the role to be played by faculties in the budgetary process.[33] Professor Cowley significantly places as the sixth and final element in good administration the statement: "Able and persuasive communication constitutes the primary factor in good administration." [34]

Manual and bylaws. A considerable body of research exists with respect to handbooks, manuals, and bylaws of boards of education responsible for elementary and secondary schools.[35] In contrast, very little energy has been devoted thus far by scholars to comparable aspects of higher education. Only two references which deal solely with this subject are cited by Eells and Hollis in their bibliography on the administration of higher education, although two other general references also deal with the subject.[36] The wide variation among boards in the practice of codifying their policies and actions into manuals and preparing written bylaws to guide their operations is evident in the response to a general request made by the U.S. Office of Education to over 2000 institutions for copies of such documents. Manuals were received from 272 of the 698 publicly controlled institutions and from 386 of the 1313 privately controlled colleges and universities. Bylaws were received from 162

---

[32] W. B. Munro, "Boards of Trustees and College Faculties," *Association of American Colleges Bulletin,* XXVII (May, 1941), 315-22.

[33] J. P. Mather, "Public Trusteeship: Pegasus or Dead Horse," *Association of Governing Boards Proceedings,* 1956, pp. 38-48.

[34] Cowley, *op. cit.,* p. 11.

[35] See for example: *Written Policies for School Boards,* American Association of School Administrators and National School Boards Association (Washington, D.C.: National Education Association, 1955).

[36] Eells and Hollis, *op. cit.,* pp. 113-17.

publicly controlled institutions and 493 privately controlled ones. Among the publicly controlled institutions, 213 reported that they did not have written bylaws and 118 so reported regarding manuals; the corresponding figures for the privately controlled colleges were 132 and 275.[37]

Contents of manuals for trustees differ considerably in accord with the functions envisioned for such a document by the board, its administrative staff, and the type of higher institution involved. The manual prepared by the staff of the New Mexico Board of Educational Finance, for example, has sections which describe the legal bases for each of the boards of control of state-operated and state-supported colleges and universities, the functions of these boards, relationships between the boards and the chief executive officers, and basic principles for effective board operation.[38] Myron Wicke, in the *Handbook for Trustees of Church-Related Colleges*, covers seven topics: the trustee system in the United States, areas of board responsibility, the relationship between the president and the board, meetings of the board, reports to the board, the trustee and faculty relationships, and the trustee and church relationships.[39] Kintzer, in analyzing the contents of 23 manuals of boards of trustees of two-year colleges, found it possible to group the 263 topics included in one or more of the documents into eight broad headings: introduction, organization of board, administration of college, professional academic staff, non-academic staff, student body and educational program, business management, buildings, equipment, grounds; and miscellaneous. He reports further that topics included in a half or more of the handbooks are concentrated in three areas: organization of board, administration of college, and academic staff.[40]

Much ambiguity is evident in the literature as to the difference between board manuals and handbooks and board bylaws. The general distinction made is that board manuals are codifications of

---

[37] As reported to the author by Dr. Archie R. Ayers, Specialist for College and University Administration, Office of Education, April 4, 1962.

[38] *Manual for Board of Regents: New Mexico State Educational Institutions* (Santa Fe, N.M.: New Mexico Board of Educational Finance, 1955).

[39] Myron F. Wicke, *Handbook for Trustees of Church-Related Colleges*, Studies in Christian Higher Education, No. 5 (Nashville, Tenn.: Methodist Board of Higher Education, 1957).

[40] Frederick C. Kintzer, *Board Policy Manuals in California Public Junior Colleges*, Occasional Report from UCLA Junior College Leadership Program, No. 2 (Los Angeles: School of Education, Junior College Leadership Program, January, 1962), pp. 9-10.

board policies on all phases of operation of the institutions under its control, whereas bylaws pertain only to rulings which are actually extensions of the legal basis or charter in matters referring specifically to the board itself—that is, board organization and duties. This distinction is implied by Elliott, Chambers, and Ashbrook in their recommendation:

> The by-laws of a board of trustees should contain all of the rules adopted by the board which are in force relating strictly to the organization and powers of the board and its methods of conducting business. Lines of authority and other relationships should be clearly set forth, important duties definitely allocated, and major responsibilities of officers and committees should be stated.[41]

Boards of trustees can resolve the ambiguity between manuals and bylaws by observing the distinction that has been set forth above. A complete set of board records, therefore, would include the basic legislation or charter from which the board initially derives its authority and responsibilities, minutes of meetings, a manual of policies currently in effect on all phases of board jurisdiction, and a set of bylaws.

Board Relationships to the Chief Executive Officer

The fact that volumes have been written about the relationships of boards of trustees of higher institutions to the president who is its chief executive officer attests to the critical character of this issue in college administration. Eells and Hollis, in a bibliography of almost 700 works on the college presidency written between 1900 and 1960, list 39 under the heading "Duties and Responsibilities to Boards of Control," and another 165 under the heading "Selection and Qualifications." [42] Since the choice of a president is overwhelmingly considered the most critical of board actions (over and over this statement is made in speeches, articles, and books),[43] the conclusion that this is a most important matter is inescapable.

---

[41] Elliott, Chambers, and Ashbrook, *op. cit.*, p. 104.

[42] Walter Crosby Eells and Ernest V. Hollis, *The College Presidency, 1900-1960: An Annotated Bibliography,* U.S. Office of Education Circular OE-53008, 1961, No. 9 (Washington, D.C.: USGPO, 1961), pp. 23-50; 95-103.

[43] See for example: Ray J. Quinlan, "President's Address," in *Proceedings,* Association of Governing Boards of State Universities and Allied Institutions, 1953, pp. 24-30; V. S. Bryant, "Responsibilities of Trustees in a State University," *College and University,* XXXIII (Fall, 1957), 13-21; and K. F. Burgess, "Trustee

Advice along three basic lines comes from the authoritative statements about board relationships with its chief executive officer. The
first is that the board, in choosing a man for the job, should start by
formulating in as clear and precise fashion as possible the kind of
executive it needs and wants, recognizing that the qualifications will
vary for different types of institutions and institutional settings. Nu-
merous studies, many subjective [44] and some objective,[45] have been
made of the college presidency and its incumbents in America. As
Carmichael observed, however: "The fact is that the background of
college presidents today in the aggregate is probably more varied
than that of any other occupation." [46] Heald establishes four broad
points for the board to keep in mind in selecting a new president:
(1) search for the best-qualified man and persuade him to accept;
(2) follow a procedure which does not embarrass either the board
or the candidates; (3) avoid a provincial point of view in selecting
a president; and (4) keep differences of view as to the qualifications
of candidates out of public disclosure and discussion.[47]

The second line of advice to boards is that the selection of a president be accomplished in cooperation with the faculty. Studies and
deliberations on the role of faculty in administration were carried
on over a period of two decades by the well-known Committee T of
the American Association of University Professors. Its final report
stated that although the answers tabulated in answer to the question, "Is the faculty consulted in the choice of a new president?"
were 60 affirmative and 148 negative in 1939, the corresponding
replies in 1953 were 112 and 111, respectively.[48]

The third line of counsel to boards is that once the choice of a
chief executive officer is made, a clear and constant separation be

Function in Today's Universities and Colleges," *Association of American Colleges
Bulletin*, XLVI (October, 1958), 399-407.

[44] See for example: William Samuel Carlson, "The Roughest Profession: The
College Presidency," *American Scholar*, XXI (Winter, 1951-52), 69-80; and Dixon
Wecter, "Prowling for Campus Presidents," *Saturday Review of Literature*, XXXI
(September 11, 1948), 9-11.

[45] See for example: Dodds, *op. cit.*

[46] Oliver C. Carmichael, "What Makes a Good College President?" *New York
Times Magazine*, September 7, 1947, p. 10.

[47] Henry T. Heald, "A Trustee's Responsibility," in *Proceedings*, Association of
Boards of State Universities and Allied Institutions, 1954, pp. 62-67.

[48] Paul William Ward, "The Place and Functions of Faculties in College and
University Administration," *AAUP Bulletin*, XLI (Spring, 1955), 62-81.

kept between the board's function of determining policies and the executive's role in general administration. Very pointed language is often used in advancing this advice. Hughes, for example, emphasizes that after the appointment of the president the board has "no more executive duties," [49] and the words of Coolidge, senior member of the Harvard Corporation, are even more graphic: "Let me emphasize one point which I think is the most important single rule for a university trustee: it is a big one, *Don't Meddle*. Don't act as an expert in education." [50]

Broad educational issues on which board attention should be heavily concentrated run the gamut of administrative subjects. Arthur Adams has suggested seven goals on which boards of trustees should be concentrating. Stated briefly, these are: reducing by one-half the number of disadvantaged but highly qualified youth who do not now continue education beyond the age of compulsory attendance; providing youth and their parents with adequate, competent, professional guidance service; examining thoroughly new learning aids, devices, and procedures and adoption of those found to be useful; mapping out a ten-year plan of community relations and public information; determining the wisest use of federal aid to education; ascertaining institutional roles in participating in overseas educational activities; and keeping the attention of the educational process focused on the importance of the individual student.[51] Although admittedly difficult to do, boards of trustees are encouraged to concentrate more heavily on such broader goals. The successful accomplishment of such goals will require a high order of leadership and the best possible policy decisions by boards of trustees.

Adherence to the principle of separation of policy formation as a primary board obligation from administrative management as a staff function does not mean a complete, arbitrary, and consequently artificial division. The principle is intended to aid board and executive communication and efficient cooperation, not to frustrate it. Thus there is help to understanding when boards study "the regent's

---

49 Raymond M. Hughes, "College and University Trustees and Their Responsibilities," *The Educational Record*, XXVI (January, 1945), 27-32.

50 Charles A. Coolidge, "Training for Trustees," *Association of American Colleges Bulletin*, XLII (December, 1956), 510-13.

51 Arthur S. Adams, "The Goals of Higher Education and the Regents Responsibility to Them," in *Proceedings*, Association of Governing Boards of State Universities and Allied Institutions, October 10-14, 1961, pp. 25-30.

role in university management," [52] and presidents make statements concerning their work as follows:

> Within the framework of the college's constitution, the annual budget, and the general policies established by the board of trustees, he must be authorized to exercise genuine authority. Otherwise, long-range planning, the development of new projects, the imaginative devising of new approaches to old problems, become impossible, and the college is trapped in a morass of administrative indecisiveness.[53]

Among the many places in the administrative process in which the chief executive officer plays a vital role is in the preparation of the agenda for board meetings. This duty, whether carried out alone or in cooperation with a board secretary, gives him recurrent opportunity to develop board understanding of institutional operations and to direct attention to needed policy determination. Particularly through agenda preparation does a president discharge what Ruml and Morrison call "a major role of the president": the development of an "informed trustee." [54] Toward this end, a president should strive toward ". . . recognizing the distinction between a legitimate sharing of problems and avoiding administrative responsibility by passing it off to the board," [55] and a trustee, in turn, should insist on coverage of each of the major phases of institutional operations in the agenda of board meetings over at least each year's sequence of sessions.

The Role of the Board in Specific Administrative Functions

"Any alert board will resist being just your 'rubber stamp.'" So the fictitious Professor I. M. Balding advised new college presidents and thereby gave the best reason for recognizing the role of the

---

[52] Ralph L. Miller, "The Regents' Role in University Management," in *Proceedings,* Association of Governing Boards of State Universities and Allied Institutions, October 10-14, 1961, pp. 41-49.

[53] Alfred F. Horrigan, "The President and His Office," *The Problems of Administration in the American College,* Roy J. Deferrari, ed. (Washington, D.C.: The Catholic University of America Press, 1956), p. 94.

[54] Ruml and Morrison, *op. cit.,* p. 77.

[55] Morton A. Rauh, *College and University Trusteeship* (Yellow Springs, Ohio: Antioch Press, 1959), p. 32.

board in specific phases of administration.[56] An effective board of trustees needs to know what is going on in institutional operations in order to make wise evaluations of past actions and to formulate judicious new ones. The following discussion takes up seven major areas of administration: formulating objectives, establishing programs, staffing, acquiring physical facilities and equipment, budgeting, interpreting the institution, and evaluating its results.

The areas of administration included in this monograph differ somewhat from those included in several other lengthy treatments of boards of trustees. Rauh, Corson, and Ruml and Morrison, for example, have a fewer number of topics under which discussion of the duties or responsibilities of the board is covered.[57] Hughes, on the other hand, includes such matters as the library, intercollegiate athletics, and fraternities and sororities.[58] The topics selected, however, include the usual and necessary steps in the administrative process from initial determination of institutional purposes to be achieved to the final evaluation of success in achieving them. The listing is similar but not identical with that accredited by Frazer to Dr. Hunter B. Blakely as steps essential to successful long-range development of higher institutions.[59]

In examining the following paragraphs, the reader should keep in mind that a separation of the administrative process into component parts is possible only in theory. In the practical administration of higher institutions, trustees, presidents, administrative staff members, and faculties work together to establish institutional purpose, implement the program, and evaluate educational outcomes. The several steps in the administrative process are often all in operation simultaneously because different problems and programs at the moment are at different stages of development.

Defining institutional purpose. The overall character of a college or university is not formed "by accident." It is the result of

---

[56] Felix C. Robb, "An Open Letter to a New College President." Address delivered at the Fifteenth Institute of Higher Education in Nashville, Tenn., July 25-27, 1960.

[57] Rauh, *op. cit.,* pp. 17-58; Corson, *op. cit.,* pp. 53-57; Ruml and Morrison, *op. cit.,* pp. 77-78.

[58] Hughes, *op. cit.,* pp. 53-138.

[59] John W. Frazer, "Long-range Planning and the Use of Government Money," in Geier, ed., *op. cit.,* pp. 87-92.

actions, planned or unplanned, taken by the administration and the faculty of the institution. Such actions over a period of time create a public image. The board of trustees has chief responsibility for determining what the image of the institution governed is to be.

This obligation derives to the board from the legal position set for it by statute or charter. Within the framework of these basic documents, the board must decide what the institution is going to accomplish, whom it is to serve, and how these goals are to be achieved. The actions taken by the president, administrative staff, and faculty should be known and accepted by the board whenever they are consistent with established institutional purposes. When actions which conflict with board conclusions are allowed to persist, a schism in administration or an unplanned change in institutional character—or both—will result.

Again, attention is called to the desirability of cooperation and interaction. As Kenneth Brown asserts: " 'We' is the proper pronoun for the academic community, in spite of the fact that it is not the pronoun most commonly heard on the campus." [60] The wise board seeks the counsel and help of its professional staff, administrative and academic, and leaders from the college constituency in making decisions about institutional goals and of development. Yet it remembers that its official responsibility for the general welfare and overall character of the institution cannot be delegated.

Determining programs of instruction, research, and service. Years of tradition lie behind the concept that the faculty controls the program of instruction of a college or university. Instruction is so closely related to the newer college functions of research, community service, and student-personnel services that these also are guarded zealously by the academic community. As a result the relative roles of faculty and administration, particularly in these matters, has become one of the most controversial issues in higher education.

Extreme positions on the issue have been taken by both administration and faculty. Francis Horn, for example, called upon administrators at all levels ". . . to unite against the common foe—the faculty!" [61] On the other hand, another administrator claims:

---

[60] Kenneth I. Brown, "The Campus As Community," *Trustee,* XV (June, 1961), 1-2.

[61] Francis H. Horn, "Academic Administrators, Unite!" *College and University Business,* XXX (June, 1961), 33.

"Administration cannot be left to the administrators. The wisdom, the experience, and the *interests* of the faculty require direct representation." [62] This position has been carried by Committee T of the American Association of University Professors to the recommendation of "... membership of faculty representatives or of other persons nominated by the faculty on the governing board. . . ." [63]

Within this field of controversy, three assignments may be given to the board of trustees: (1) maintenance of a sense of direction and balance in institutional offerings consistent with educational purposes; (2) recognition and preservation of the values of academic freedom in instruction, research, and service and of faculty involvement in developing policies in these realms; and (3) encouragement of change in institutional offerings as conditions change.

Consistent with the first assignment would be an alertness on the part of the trustees to both the direction and degree of change in the institutional program of offerings. The suggestions advanced by Ruml and Morrison to liberal colleges for establishment of a mechanism which involves trustees, administration, and faculty for curriculum examination and control may well be heeded also by trustees of other types of institutions.[64]

The essence of the second assignment is in the fact that it must be carried out to protect the integrity of institutions of higher learning as centers of free inquiry and discussion. In this the trustees have a vital function to perform. The threat has been phrased well by Abbott:

> I believe that the most critical problem that we in higher education must solve in the years ahead—faculty members, boards, presidents, and 'bureaucrats' alike—is to develop and maintain public understanding of the social role of the college and university as a free, critical, creative, not necessarily conforming agent, which in a free society must be maintained as such against pressures for conformity to particular conventions, attitudes, loyalties.[65]

---

62 Harold W. Stoke, *The American College Presidency* (New York: Harper & Row, Publishers, 1959), p. 123.

63 "Faculty Participation in College and University Government," *AAUP Bulletin,* XLII (Summer, 1960), 203-4.

64 Ruml and Morrison, *op. cit.,* p. 14.

65 Frank Abbott, "Critique: The Role of Faculty in College Administration," in *Studies of College Faculty* (Boulder, Colo.: Western Interstate Commission for Higher Education, and Berkeley, Calif.: University of California, The Center for the Study of Higher Education, December, 1961), p. 103.

As long ago as 1935, an eminent university president observed that the bastions of academic freedom were being held predominantly by the faculty and the American Association of University Professors. He contended then that the trustees also had an obligation in this area.[66] The obligation is a constant one and alert trustees will fulfill their part in preserving the integrity and freedom of higher learning.

Attention was called above to the fact that institutions have an inherent tendency to expand. Paradoxically, there exists on the usual campus also a basic conservatism toward change, sometimes even when changes are consistent with institutional purposes and are demanded by new conditions. In such situations, as Mather and others have advised, a responsible trusteeship must, as an obligation of the office, encourage change when it is justified.[67] In doing so, however, the better procedure, as Ruml and Morrison suggest, is to secure as much support and enthusiasm for the change as can possibly be achieved.[68]

Staffing the institution. Because "a college is only as good as its faculty," development of the best possible staff is a prime objective in institutional administration. Whether or not the goal is attained depends in large measure on the policies for staffing that are set up by the board of trustees. The faculty, the administrative staff, and the chief executive officer need to advance to the board policy recommendations concerning the recruitment and retention of staff. As the reviewing and officially approving agency, however, the board has ultimate control over the excellence and effectiveness of the personnel policy that eventuates. Referring to this matter, Capen wrote:

> . . . the trustees are the employers. As employers they determine the principles and the policy of employment. If the employment policy is an enlightened one, a university can attract and hold able teachers. With their aid it can grow in strength and reputation. If

66 Samuel P. Capen, "Responsibility of Boards of Trustees for the Preservation of Academic Freedom," *American Association of University Professors Bulletin,* XXI (October, 1935), 477-82.

67 J. P. Mather, "Public Trusteeship: Pegasus or Dead Horse," in *Proceedings,* Association of Governing Boards of State Universities and Allied Institutions, 1956, 38-48.

68 Ruml and Morrison, *op. cit.,* p. 56.

the policy is oppressive a university can get only second or third raters on its teaching staff.[69]

Much has been written as to the specifics that should be put in a good faculty personnel policy.[70] The end result sought in these in broad terms is a high faculty and staff morale, a state that contributes significantly to educational accomplishments on the campus. To attain this kind of staff morale, it is not enough to have a forward-looking policy on such matters as salaries, fringe benefits, teaching load, and the like; the board must also have a courageous policy that seeks out the able teacher and protects his freedom to perform his task of instruction and research. Repeatedly, writings stress this basic principle; the board of trustees must stand behind the competent scholar who is doing his job well, even in the face of controversy and public examination.[71]

In this connection and related also to comments made earlier in this chapter concerning board bylaws, the recommendation of a committee of the American Council on Education on faculty-administration relationships may be a worthwhile idea for individual boards to adopt:

> Prepare a descriptive report concerning college and university statutes and bylaws for faculty, board, and administrative officers, with a statement of principles to guide the development and maintenance of such statutes and bylaws. Contents might include (a) charters and bylaws; (b) statutes general to the college or university; (c) faculty "constitutions" and operating procedures; (d) budget procedures.[72]

Acquiring and protecting needed physical facilities and equipment. In a time of rising enrollments and public demands for the services of higher educational institutions, there is likely to be pres-

---

[69] Samuel P. Capen, *The Management of Universities, op. cit.,* p. 35.

[70] More than 500 references dealing with the topics, "Recruitment and Appointment," "Qualifications," "Status," and "Working Conditions," are cited by Eells and Hollis, *Administration of Higher Educaton, op. cit.,* pp. 154-222.

[71] See for example: "The Role of College and University Trustees," *North Central Association Quarterly,* XXVIII (January, 1954), 290-97; Laird Bell, "From the Trustee's Corner," *Association of American Colleges Bulletin,* XLII (October, 1956), 353-61; and I. L. Kandel, "Trustees and Investigations in Colleges and Universities," *School and Society,* LXXVII (May 7, 1953), 153.

[72] Frank C. Abbott, ed., *Faculty-Administration Relationships,* Report of a Work Conference, May 7-9, 1957, sponsored by the Commission on Instruction and Evaluation of the American Council on Education (Washington, D.C.: American Council on Education, 1958), p. 88.

ent also an expanding need for physical facilities and equipment. This will characterize higher education in America at least during the next fifty years. Private supporters of colleges and universities, as well as local, state, and federal governments, are being called upon to increase their activity in support of higher institutions, and in many instances specifically in the area of buildings and equipment.

In this area boards of trustees have three functions to perform. First, they must be sure that a clear and complete assessment of institutional needs for buildings and equipment has been made and is being kept up to date. Secondly, they must decide on policies to govern procedures for acquiring the needed facilities; that is, decisions as to where and how the money will be acquired, and the time schedule for getting it. Thirdly, once the facilities are obtained the board has the legal obligations of ownership, that is, making certain that it is used, cared for, and protected properly.

The nature of the policies to be established by a particular board of trustees will depend on a number of factors. Publicly supported institutions, in comparison to privately controlled ones, for example, will arrive at different decisions in the way new facilities will be financed.

The point to be made here is that an active and alert board is "ahead of the game" in building and campus planning as it is in other areas of administrative planning. It does not wait for situations of pressure or crisis to develop but anticipates new developments and formulates policies to meet them. A caution, however, is in order in the realm of planning for buildings and equipment: there is danger that undue energy of the board will be exerted. The discussion on board committees above mentioned buildings and grounds as one matter to which a standing committee of the board was often assigned. Sometimes the requirements imposed by statutes and building regulations force this degree of attention on the part of the board.[73] To the extent possible, however, a board of trustees should concentrate on formulating sound policies for planning, financing, use, and preservation of buildings and equipment and delegate the implementation of these policies to the employed professional staff.

---

[73] Martorana, Hollis, *et al., op. cit.,* Vol. I, pp. 32-33.

Budgeting and financing. Ideally, the question of acquiring needed funds comes after determination of purposes, program, staff needs, and physical facilities required. Adherence to this procedure by trustees is to be recommended in principle, even though in practical operations the question of financing appears to precede and supersede all others.

Realistically reviewed, budgeting as a part of board responsibility is an important part of both short-range and long-range planning. Corson describes how it operates in the immediate planning situation:

> The annual budget is in effect a fiscal statement of the institution's educational program. By setting salary levels for the faculty, the board influences the caliber of the educational offering. In determining what physical facilities shall be provided, in choosing between laboratories or dormitories, a student union building and a classroom building, the board similarly influences the educational program.[74]

The relationship between budgeting and long-range planning is described as follows by Ralph Hetzel, a trustee of The Pennsylvania State University:

> A proper companion for a long-range plan is a long-range budget. . . . I think the plan and budget should be specifically projected at least ten years ahead and broadly projected another decade. They need to be re-examined and re-adjusted constantly. The mirage of the perfected university changes and moves off when approached.[75]

In elaborating the point, Hetzel suggests use of a long-range budget such as has been projected by Tickton and others. The plan presented includes procedures for working out such a budget and background information justifying their use. Evidence is growing that this counsel to boards of trustees is being followed at an increasing rate.[76]

---

[74] Corson, *op. cit.,* p. 55.

[75] Ralph Hetzel, "What Are the Central Responsibilities of the Trustee Which Apply Both to Publicly and Privately Supported Institutions?" in *Current Issues in Higher Education,* 1960 (Washington, D.C.: Association for Higher Education, National Education Association, 1960), p. 154.

[76] Sidney G. Tickton, *Needed: A Ten Year College Budget* (New York: The Fund for the Advancement of Education, 1961), p. 13; and Dexter M. Keezer, *Financing Higher Education, 1960-70* (New York: McGraw-Hill Book Company, 1959), Chapter 7.

In the general field of financing, trustees are looked to perform two primary functions. One is to assist personally in the acquisition of necessary funds. This does not necessarily mean that the trustee himself is expected to contribute heavily to the institution, but his leadership should be evident in the total effort to acquire funds. In the case of publicly controlled institutions, this involves the board of trustees' cooperation in developing sound understanding of the institution on the part of members of the legislature, the governor, and other civic leaders. Among privately controlled institutions, it involves effort in fund drives and related efforts of a planned nature to secure funds.[77]

The second major function of trustees is the actual care and supervision of funds owned by the institution. Here the legal responsibility of the trustees is clear and there is generally little delegation of this function. Trustees usually handle not only policies governing investments, but also the selection of securities in which funds are to be placed.[78] That this close control on investments and of transactions involving real property is wise and proper is evident in the writings on college financing. Russell identified six different agencies, including the board as a whole, that are commonly engaged in management of a college's endowment and evaluated each in terms of usefulness for colleges of various types and endowments of different magnitudes.[79] The general recommendation, however, is that wherever possible the trustees seek the assistance of professional investment counsel in this matter and require periodic and critical review of the investment plan and financial holdings of the institution.[80]

Interpreting the institution to the public. That trustees have a role to perform in making their colleges better known to the public is another point on which a strong consensus exists among

---

[77] Arnaud C. Marts, "The Place of Trustees in 'Tested Methods of Organizing Solicitation Assistance,'" *Association of American Colleges Bulletin,* XL (October, 1954), 409-11; and D. P. Reed, "Board Member: Keystone of Philanthropy," *Association of American Colleges Bulletin,* XXX (May, 1949), 361-67.

[78] Rauh, *op. cit.,* p. 47.

[79] John Dale Russell, *The Finance of Higher Education,* rev. ed. (Chicago: The University of Chicago Press, 1954), pp. 276-79.

[80] See for example: T. Arnett, "College Trustee and College Finance," *Association of American Colleges Bulletin,* XXV (May, 1939), 320-25; William E. Camp, "Have You Considered Compiling an Endowment Digest?" *College and University Business,* XVII (September, 1954), 45; and J. Harvey Cain, "Long-Term Investing," *College and University Business,* XXII (August, 1957), 22-23.

scholars in the field. The role to be played appears to be a twofold one. First, the trustees are expected to join with the other responsible segments of the academic community in presenting and keeping what Tead calls "the institution's good name" [81] before its constituency and all segments of the general public that may have an interest in the college. A concise definition of public relations and the trustee's role in this team concept is set forth by Snider:

> Public relations is really the impression we make on others and the effects of those impressions on them and on ourselves. . . . Public relations is definitely not a one-man affair. It is a team-job and must be considered as such. To share most fully in this team-job, every trustee must endeavor to carry out his own responsibilities so that his college will be making impressions that do two things: (1) win and retain the good will of the college's various publics, and (2) lead its publics to express their good will in words, actions and activities which will bring to the college increasing strength and recognition. The role of the trustee is an important one, and public relations must see that he is truly a part of the over-all picture.[82]

Though addressed to trustees of a particular group of colleges, the counsel Snider advanced is appropriate also for trustees of other higher institutions. If the differences in institutional purposes and consequent characteristics of program are understood and kept in mind, the techniques and goals of public relations are commonly applicable to all kinds of higher institutions. "Good public relations in junior colleges," wrote Jesse P. Bogue, for example, "is not essentially different from that in any other type of higher educational institution." [83]

There are times, however, when the role of the trustee in institutional public relations must be discharged by individual trustees or by the trustees acting officially as a corporate body. When individual trustees perform these tasks, they serve in a manner termed by Gerber as "ambassador" for the institution and its welfare.[84] Corson describes instances when the board of trustees officially and publicly

---

81 Ordway Tead, "College Trustees: Their Opportunities and Duties," *Journal of Higher Education*, XXII (April, 1951), 171-80.

82 Jack E. Snider, "Public Relations for a Church College," in Geier, ed., *op. cit.*, p. 52.

83 Jesse P. Bogue, "The Functions of Good Public Relations in Junior Colleges," *Junior College Journal*, XXVIII (December, 1957), 223-228.

84 J. Jay Gerber, "The Trustee's Job in the Development Program," *College and University Business*, XXVI (March, 1959), 44-45.

supported actions that had been taken by the institutions and had come into public question and discussion. In these instances, he reports, ". . . only the distinguished representatives of the public who serve on the board could speak to defend the institution." [85]

Evaluating the institution and its program. Institutions of higher learning, like all other enterprises, are not equally successful in accomplishing the purposes set for them. Trustees need therefore to establish plans and techniques whereby institutional effectiveness can be determined objectively and regularly. On the basis of outcomes from such evaluation, earlier policies and decisions can be reappraised and new ones established.

In this area of administrative responsibility, perhaps even more than in the others discussed above, the trustees do not themselves enter into the process. Their duty is to see that the evaluation takes place and that results become available for use by the board. The actual conduct of studies and surveys is the duty of the regular staff of the college or of outside specialists employed by the board. The latter practice, using private educational and management consultants, university professors of higher education, and agencies of the state and federal government, is on the increase.[86] Institutional evaluation is going on almost constantly in connection with such matters as the acquisition of accreditation of the institution or of programs offered by the institution, examination of the credit status of the institution as a part of the process of seeking a loan or issuing bonds, appraisal of the level of demand of students for admission to the college, and the ease or difficulty encountered in recruiting and holding competent faculty members. These matters need to be known to the board and used especially in appraising the success and validity of the administrative counsel it is receiving.

Though the trustees themselves will not likely be involved in the actual conduct of evaluative studies, they ought to be acquainted with the approaches that are used in these projects and aware of the fact that they are being conducted in increasing numbers.[87] A study

---

[85] Corson, *op. cit.,* p. 57.

[86] S. V. Martorana and James C. Messersmith, *Advance Planning to Meet Higher Education Needs, Recent State Studies, 1956-59,* U.S. Office of Education Circular No. 633 (Washington, D.C.: USGPO, 1960), pp. 2-7.

[87] A few notable exceptions can be found to the generalization that trustees generally are not directly involved in the conduct of evaluative studies. One example is the participation by the Board of Trustees in the Educatonal Survey of the University of Pennsylvania and reported by Donald R. Belcher, *The Board of Trustees*

and review of writings in this field indicates four approaches that seem to be used predominantly in the evaluation of higher institutions. These approaches could be enumerated and designated as: (1) direct determination of educational effectiveness, (2) the management analysis approach, (3) the sociological approach, and (4) the psychological approach. The first is illustrated by the efforts of the North Central Association of Colleges and Secondary Schools, a major national accrediting association, to relate the operations of a higher institution to the stated objectives which the institution is supposed to attain. In this approach, effort has been made to identify criteria of excellence and measures which correlate positively or otherwise portray as objectively as possible the degree of educational success reached by the institution.[88] The second approach utilizes a rationale and methodology closer to the techniques of business and industrial management analysis, whereby relatively specific, definable aspects of institutional operations are selected for more penetrating study and appraisal. This approach is commonly found in institutional self-studies and in some statewide studies where such matters as faculty-student credit-hour production, instructional unit costs, and space utilization are studied quite intensively.[89] In these studies, as in studies using the other approaches, of course, the results are compiled to appraise as much as possible the overall effectiveness of the institution.

The sociological approach to institutional study uses quite a different method, concentrating on the attributes of the college as a social institution or as a culture in itself. The results provide a basis for appraising the atmosphere and setting in which the academic enterprise takes place and thus an indirect indication of likelihood of success in achieving educational objectives. This is the method

---

of *The University of Pennsylvania* (Philadelphia: University of Pennsylvania Press, 1957).

[88] See for example: Russell and Reeves, *Evaluation of Higher Institutions, op. cit.* A series of monographs based on the investigation conducted for the Committee on Revision of Standards, Commission on Higher Institutions of the North Central Association of Colleges and Secondary Schools.

[89] Examples of this approach are found in A. J. Brumbaugh and Morris W. H. Collins, Jr., *University of Georgia Study, Final Report* (Athens, Ga.: University of Georgia, 1958); Lyman A. Glenny, *The Nebraska Study of Higher Education* (Lincoln, Neb.: Legislative Council, 1961); and T. R. McConnell, T. C. Holy, and H. H. Semans, *A Restudy of the Needs of California in Higher Education* (Sacramento, Calif.: State Department of Education, 1955).

employed in such studies as *The Academic Man,* by Logan Wilson [90] and *The Open Door College,* by Burton R. Clark.[91] This method is inherent also in the analysis and writings of W. H. Cowley, which develop the proposition that colleges and universities are subcultures which operate within larger cultures, and that these external and internal cultures intermesh and control the activities of higher institutions.[92]

With the advancement of psychological theories and instruments for studying human behavior, there has appeared most recently the fourth method of institutional appraisal identified above. Here attempt is made to determine the peculiarities of institutional "personality" or "mind" that results from the collective minds and personalities of the persons associated with the institution.[93] Instruments such as standardized interviews, tests, and scales have been used to determine the characteristics of colleges as perceived by students,[94] the attitudes of faculty,[95] and the impact of the college's environment on student learning, personality, and growth.[96]

In concluding this chapter, attention is called again to the basic point that effectiveness in administration and in institutional operations in general requires a strong cooperative effort by trustees, the president, the administrative staff, and the faculty. The proper idea is expressed well by President Emeritus Morrill of Minnesota, who said:

> None of the groups in the American university community—the trustee, the administration, the faculty, or the students—is self-contained or, in practice, fully self-governing. Each has responsi-

---

[90] Logan Wilson, *The Academic Man, A Study in the Sociology of a Profession* (New York: Oxford University Press, 1942).

[91] Burton R. Clark, *The Open Door College: A Case Study* (New York: McGraw-Hill Book Company, 1960).

[92] W. H. Cowley, *Appraisal of American Higher Education* (unpublished manuscript, 1956) as cited in E. D. Duryea, "Institutional Personality," *The Educational Record,* XLII (October, 1961), 330-35.

[93] H. S. Person, "The Institutional Mind," *Advanced Management* (December, 1956), as cited by E. D. Duryea, *op. cit.,* p. 332.

[94] James W. Wilson and Edwards H. Lyons, *Work-Study College Programs: Appraisal and Report of the Study of Cooperative Education* (New York: Harper & Row, Publishers, 1961), pp. 27-40.

[95] Joseph Katz, "Personality and Interpersonal Relations in the Classroom," in Nevitt Sanford, ed., *The American College: A Psychological and Social Interpretation of the Higher Learning* (New York: John Wiley & Sons, 1962), pp. 365-95.

[96] "Research in Progress," *The American College and Student Personality: Report of a Conference on College Influences on Personality* (Andover, Mass.: Social Science Research Council, March, 1959), pp. 1-4.

bilities to the other; each needs communication and cooperation with the other; each is sometimes dissatisfied with its place in the sphere of things. As in any democratic enterprise, the problems of government, including university government, are never quite resolved. But the basic relationship remains a cooperative and not an autocratic one, emphasizing the voluntary nature of the University enterprise, in which any form of arbitrary administration is incompatible with success.[97]

Corson devised a schematic diagram to show the role of the president as the center of power in his institution.[98] Adapting the idea to the role of the board of trustees in cooperative effort with other elements of the academic community in carrying on each of the seven areas of administration discussed above, the relations indicated by the shaded areas in the accompanying chart are suggested:

THE ROLE OF THE TRUSTEES

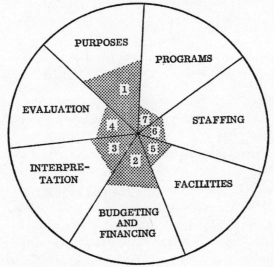

---

[97] J. L. Morrill, *The On-Going State University* (Minneapolis, Minn.: University of Minnesota Press, 1960), p. 49.
[98] Corson, *op. cit.*, p. 71.

CHAPTER V

A Look to the Future

The structure for administration of colleges and universities can be expected to change in the future, as it has in the past, to adjust to new conditions in higher education. A look to the future of college boards of trustees, therefore, must attempt to assay those factors which appear to be most likely to produce changes in the administration of higher learning that in turn will bear upon the role of the board. Two types of forces toward change are discussed below: first, those which would tend to take from boards of trustees some of their traditional duties and powers of control over higher institutions; and, second, those that would change the character of the membership of these boards from their historical layman composition.

Current Concern for
Autonomy of Boards of Trustees

During the late 1950's and early 1960's, a concern for the rights of boards of trustees to govern higher education that had been developing for many years greatly intensified. The concern was expressed in the term "erosion of board control" and attracted attention of both individual researchers and special study groups. Some who studied the development concluded that gradual loss of board authority would lead ultimately to abandonment of the trustee structure.[1] Others, although concluding that some changes would likely emerge, did not lend support to such a drastic prediction.[2]

Notable among the efforts of special study groups bearing on the question of erosion of board authority was the Committee on Gov-

---

[1] Herman Lee Donovan, "The Vanishing University Trustee," *Peabody Educational Journal,* XXXVI (March, 1954), 259-63.

[2] See for example: Lyman A. Glenny, *Autonomy of Public Colleges: The Challenge of Coordination* (New York: McGraw-Hill Book Company, 1959), pp. 263-67; M. M. Chambers, *Voluntary Statewide Coordination in Public Higher Education* (Ann Arbor, Mich.: The University of Michigan Press, 1961), pp. 48-57; and S. V. Martorana and Ernest V. Hollis, *State Boards Responsible for Higher Education,* U.S. Office of Education Circular No. 619 (Washington, D.C.: USGPO, 1960), pp. 47-53.

ernment and Higher Education which was appointed in 1957 to make a thorough inquiry into the status of state-supported colleges and universities within the larger context of state government. Sponsored jointly by the Association of Governing Boards of State Universities and Allied Institutions, the National Association of State Universities, and the American Association of State Universities and Land-Grant Colleges, the study culminated in two reports that are landmarks in asserting the case for preservation of board autonomy and authority.[3]

Erosion of board control and authority. The collective efforts of studies such as these accumulated much evidence that the powers of boards of trustees as governing bodies of colleges and universities had indeed been reduced in many states and in several important areas. This outcome may be attributed to the concurrence of two developments: the considerable expansion and strengthening of the agencies of state government—particularly those usually attached to the executive branch—that has taken place during the past fifty years, and the great upsurge of public interest in and demand for higher education that began with the "G. I. Bulge" after World War II. Rapidly increasing enrollments produced larger budgetary demands for higher institutions, both for operating expenses and for capital facilities. State governments began to rely increasingly on such executive agencies as departments of administration or finance, budget bureaus, central purchasing offices, civil service or personnel commissions, state building authorities, and state auditors to examine and keep check on the growth and development of higher education. Legislatures established special committees on higher education and called for special studies and reports by legislative reference bureaus or research councils. As boards of trustees of publicly controlled institutions found themselves having to deal more and more with these agencies, and often having to go through them to the governor and legislature, the erosion of board autonomy and control was felt and its nature described.

The heightened interaction of state-supported institutions and state governments that has been described for the 1950's and early 1960's appears likely to continue for some time. Moreover, the

---

[3] Malcolm Moos and Francis E. Rourke, *The Campus and the State;* and Committee on Government and Higher Education, *The Efficiency of Freedom* (Baltimore, Md.: The Johns Hopkins Press, 1959).

privately controlled colleges may prove also to be affected, although less directly than those operating under public auspices. During the period mentioned, the pressures of enrollment expansion and increases in operating costs were met largely by the individual institutions and by newly created voluntary organizations such as the Council for the Advancement of Small Colleges and the Council for Financial Aid to Higher Education—agencies intended to help colleges, both public and private, find the necessary resources to grow in size and services. Despite such voluntary and privately sponsored efforts, some states and the federal government deemed it necessary to establish, in the interest of both the states and the nation, programs which bear directly and indirectly on the operations of public and private colleges. Thus, for example, New York State established in 1961 a "scholar incentive program," [4] adding to a state scholarship program which has been emulated by many other states. In 1958 Congress enacted the National Defense Education Act, with four titles that relate directly to higher education.[5]

In all these programs a notable effort was extended to assure the continued autonomy of the colleges and their boards of trustees and to avoid state or federal control of institutional policies or operations. In this objective they have overwhelmingly succeeded. Nevertheless, to the extent that boards of trustees which take advantage of such programs must report and account for funds and related matters to other agencies, they are less free and independent than before.

In the United States, privately controlled colleges and universities have historically been exempt from taxation by public jurisdictions. This has in no way caused encroachments by public authority on the operation of these institutions. During the 1950's and the early 1960's, however, there appeared, perhaps more than in any comparable period in earlier times, discussion as to the implications of the tax exemption privilege on the responsibilities for public service of the institutions involved.[6] What direction this heightened discus-

---

[4] New York State Session Laws, 1961, Chapter 389.

[5] Public Law 85-864, September 2, 1958. Title II: Loans to Students in Institutions of Higher Education; Title IV: National Defense Fellowships; Title V, B: Counseling and Guidance Training Institutes; Title VI: Language Development.

[6] See for example: T. E. Blackwell, "How State Laws May Restrict College Admissions Practices," *College and University Business,* XXXII (May, 1962), 86-88; and "Tulane Decision May Have Wide Impact," Association of State Universities and Land-Grant Colleges Circular Letter No. 9 (mimeographed), April 4, 1962, Washington, D.C.

sion will take as far as the issue of board autonomy is concerned cannot now be determined.

Countering efforts.   Attempts to preserve the traditional autonomy and completeness of authority of governing boards for the operation of colleges and universities have taken four lines of approach. The four approaches may be described topically as: (1) organized effort to identify, describe, and counteract systematically factors which contribute to the erosion of board autonomy; (2) effort to acquire more safeguards for the authority of boards of publicly controlled institutions in state constitutional provisions; (3) greater attention to voluntary coordination and inter-institutional cooperation among governing boards and their institutions; and (4) development of new types of formal and official administrative structures for the administration of higher education. These seek to keep the important functions of coordination, long-range planning, research and fact-finding, and policy formation concerning inter-institutional affairs in the hands of persons concerned with and responsible for higher education rather than those primarily concerned with other aspects of state government.

An excellent illustration of the first approach cited above is found in the establishment of a special Committee on Legislation and Inter-Governmental Relations by the Association of Governing Boards of State Universities and Allied Institutions. This committee has responsibility to identify encroachments upon board authority and to make annual reports to the executive committee and membership of the Association as to the nature of these encroachments and actions that might be taken to counteract them.

Extension of provisions in state constitutions to guarantee the autonomy of boards of trustees of publicly controlled institutions is handicapped by the difficulties that are usually attached to revision of these documents. The recommendation that such constitutional amendments be sought appears often in statewide studies and surveys of higher education,[7] and M. M. Chambers asserts that this is the surest technique for the preservation of board authority and autonomy.[8] Illustrations of recent instances in which constitutional

---

[7] See for example: John Dale Russell, *Higher Education in Michigan*. The final report of the survey of higher education in Michigan (Lansing, Mich.: Michigan Legislative Study Committee on Higher Education, 1958), p. 114.

[8] Chambers, *op. cit.*, p. 41.

freedoms and powers have been granted to state institutions in a manner and extent comparable to that held by the major institutions in Michigan are rare. In this connection, it is of interest to note that the two newest states, Hawaii and Alaska, though both creating a state university by constitutional provision, do not grant extensive autonomy to the board of regents for the administration of these institutions. In both cases, the legislatures have significant statutory controls over them.

During the period following World War II through the 1960's, a greater tendency for the administrations of colleges and universities voluntarily to coordinate their efforts and programs was evident.[9] This, as has been noted, was in part owing to the pressures of enrollment expansions and increases in costs of operation. Evidence is strong also that it was in part the result of recognition by the leadership in higher education that this was necessary to protect the role in the administration of colleges and universities. This is evident in the factors surrounding the emergence and strengthening of such organizations as the Ohio Inter-University Council, the Michigan Council of State College Presidents, and the Colorado Association of State-Supported Institutions, as described by M. M. Chambers.[10]

Evidence to support the fourth of the approaches stated for counteracting moves toward reducing board authority and freedom is found in the increasing number of states that have established statewide boards for purposes of coordinating higher institutions, but without governing powers over them. With the close of the 1961 legislative year, there were ten states that had taken such action. In that same year Arkansas established a Commission on Coordination of Higher Educational Finance.[11] This agency is to coordinate the finances of the Arkansas state-supported higher institutions and their eight different governing boards.[12] In his discussion of "the constructive role of coordination," T. R. McConnell makes a statement that holds special significance for boards of trustees that are

[9] S. V. Martorana, James C. Messersmith, and Lawrence O. Nelson, *Cooperative Projects Among Colleges and Universities,* U.S. Office of Education Circular No. 649 (Washington, D.C.: USGPO, 1961), p. 5.

[10] Chambers, *op. cit.,* pp. 18-43.

[11] S. V. Martorana, "Statewide Coordination of Higher Education: Plans, Surveys, and Progress to Date," *Current Issues in Higher Education, 1962* (Washington, D.C.: Association for Higher Education, National Education Association, 1962), pp. 245-48.

[12] Act 24 of the 1st Extraordinary Session, 1961.

concerned with the preservation of their autonomy and authority and the relationship of these goals to interinstitutional coordination. He says:

> The debates and actions concerning coordination in the several states have made the basic issue clear: the choice between formal and voluntary bodies and procedures involves a balancing of values, and the values of independence, initiative, and responsibility weigh heavily in the quest for institutional excellence and integrity. The end to be gained is a *productive* compromise between the values of autonomy and coordination.
>
> The writer is not yet ready to concede that voluntary coordination cannot meet the need for cooperative planning, definition of institutional roles and relationships, and integrity in carrying out agreements. Of one thing he is certain, however; if voluntary methods fail—and they will not have much time to prove their effectiveness—formal coordinating methods are inevitable.[13]

The argument in favor of some structured approach to the coordination of higher institutions, either voluntary or formal and official, is that it accomplishes the goals usually sought by the executive and legislative arms of state government while retaining control of higher educational affairs in boards and professional personnel who have a close interest in and understanding of higher institutions. Consensus is strong among authorities in higher education that interinstitutional coordination is a growing necessity and that the basic issue is not whether or not there will be such coordination, but what agency will provide this service. Thus, if it is not accomplished successfully by the higher education community itself, the function will be performed by some departmental agency of state government or the legislature itself.

The Ideal Objective— Lay Boards and Professional Staffs

Throughout this monograph attention has been called to the basic principle that boards of trustees for the administration of higher institutions should be composed of laymen. Through application of this idea from the earliest days of American higher education an effective separation of roles has evolved and become recognized for

---

[13] T. R. McConnell, *A General Pattern for American Public Higher Education* (New York: McGraw-Hill Book Company, 1962), pp. 161-62.

its advantages to both the institution and the constituency it serves. Boards of trustees set the policies for institutional operations while the professional staff manage the colleges and the academic process. To this principle there is general and overwhelming agreement in the literature on college and university administration. The principle is valid for both types of boards of trustees which govern institutions, and the logic behind it is easily extended to hold for boards which are responsible for interinstitutional coordination. Yet it must be reported that the principle has been challenged and reasons advanced for departing from its use.

Lay boards of trustees for institutions. Changes of two types in board composition seem most likely if modification of the principle of lay membership is to occur. One of these would add members who represent the faculty, and the other would extend membership to the president of the institution.

One of the strongest criticisms voiced against the basic idea of use of lay boards of trustees is that these bodies lack clear understanding of the academic community and fail to maintain adequate communications with the faculty. Adherents to this view argue for faculty representation on the board. Although as a general rule relatively little support for this position is found in the literature outside of the publications of the American Association of University Professors,[14] some indications of compromise are to be found. Thus, for example, Beck, suggesting a model university board structure which he describes as applicable also to colleges, boards of education of public schools, and state boards of education, proposes thirteen members described as follows:

8 representatives of *The Public* (at least one of whom should be a woman), distributed as follows:
   2 representatives of business, broadly defined
   2 representatives of the professions
   2 representatives of agriculture
   2 representatives of wage earners

5 representatives of *The University* (at least one of whom should be a woman), distributed as follows:
   2 representatives of the faculty

---

[14] See for example: Max Savelle, "Democratic Government of the State University: A Proposal," *Bulletin of the AAUP,* XLIII (June, 1957), 323-28; and R. J. Alexander, "Should the Faculty Run the Board of Trustees?" *American Teacher,* XXXVIII (December, 1953), 14-15.

2 representatives of the alumni
1 representative of the students [15]

Several arguments can be advanced in favor of making the president of the institution a member of the board. Among these would be that the practice is common in industry and business and another is that it guarantees that the chief executive will be fully aware of board actions and attitudes.

Thus far in the history of higher education in America, pressures for modifying the layman structure of boards of trustees either to include members of the faculty or the president of the institution have not prevailed. In contrast, extensive documentation of reasons for not doing so can be found. One writer, for example, asserts that faculty representation on the board of trustees puts the person concerned in a very difficult professional position, detracts from his primary job of research and instruction, and creates misunderstandings between faculty and administration about the primary locus of responsibility for policy.[16] Equally pointed comment against inclusion of the president as a board member has appeared, one of the most direct from two former presidents of state universities.[17]

The fundamental concept of lay representation on boards of trustees is becoming more accepted even among some church-related, privately controlled higher institutions that for many years have operated without this type of board. Stanford states that boards that are controlled by religious orders are archaic and should be supplanted by separate boards that include laymen, though he does not carry this recommendation to the total composition of the board.[18]

Whether or not it will become necessary in future years to depart from the traditional practice of lay board membership in this country will in large measure depend on the actions of the trustees themselves. Boards of trustees should make a concerted effort to understand the academic community, to maintain effective liaison

[15] Hubert Park Beck, *Men Who Control Our Universities* (New York: King's Crown Press, 1947), p. 151.

[16] Harry J. Carman, "Board of Trustees and Regents," in *Administrators in Higher Education: Their Functions and Coordination,* Gerald P. Burns, ed. (New York: Harper & Row, Publishers, 1962), pp. 83-84.

[17] Frank L. McVey and Raymond M. Hughes, *Problems of College and University Administration* (Ames, Iowa: The Iowa State College Press, 1952), pp. 64-65.

[18] E. V. Stanford, "Functional Board of Trustees for the Catholic College," *Catholic Education Review,* LIX (February, 1961), 102-7.

with the faculty, and to establish as a matter of standard operating policy the practice of having the chief executive officer present at all meetings except those at which his status with the board and his salary are discussed. If this is done, the main arguments for varying from lay membership of boards of control will be obviated and the dangers that inhere in having salaried personnel of the institution as members of the board avoided.

Lay boards for statewide and inter-institutional coordination. In the main, boards of higher education which carry responsibility for governing and coordinating groups of publicly controlled colleges show in their membership structure the same adherence to laymen representation as do the governing boards. A notably smaller emphasis on lay representation was found, however, in the case of statewide boards that function only to provide overall coordination and planning for higher education. Approximately 25 percent of the total membership of the eight statewide coordinating boards operating in 1959 was determined *ex officio*. A striking fact in this finding was that three out of ten of the *ex officio* membership on these boards were presidents of the institutions involved in the coordination program and almost half were members of boards of control of the institutions covered.[19]

From these facts and from the general discussion in the literature and at professional meetings where the subject of coordination is examined comes the clear conclusion that presidents of colleges and universities, and indeed members of their boards of trustees, are as eager for a voice and representation on boards whose duties affect their operations as faculty members are for representation on institutional boards of trustees. Whether or not a heavy or complete representation of institutional interests ought to exist in the makeup of a coordinating board depends on the extent that the coordination is to be viewed as "voluntary." If the institutional leaders are expected to coordinate themselves, good arguments can be advanced for the board to be made up of official representatives of the institutions involved.

The legal provisions establishing statewide coordinating boards vary greatly in this regard. At one extreme, for example, is the

---

[19] Martorana and Hollis, *op. cit.*, p. 26.

eighteen-man Council on Public Higher Education in Kentucky which includes all of the presidents of state-supported higher institutions in the state, members of the boards of these institutions, the dean of the State University College of Education, the superintendent of public instruction, and two members of the state board of education. At the other extreme are the nine-man North Carolina Board of Higher Education and the fifteen-member Commission on Higher Education in Texas, both founded on legal statements which have strong stipulations that the representation of the board must be of persons not professionally engaged in higher education.[20] Significant to note in this is the action of the 1962 Kentucky Legislature which amended the membership structure of the Council on Public Higher Education to include "three additional lay members from the state-at-large to be appointed by the governor." [21]

The existence of statewide coordinating boards that are predominantly composed of lay persons and others that are made up wholly, or largely, of representatives of the institutions involved in the coordination program is fortuitous for research into the pattern that is best suited to the needs of higher education in the nation. More critical examinations along the lines of Glenny's study [22] and Chambers' review [23] can be made. Thus an objective determination can be made that will provide better guidelines for the composition of new coordinating boards and the reconstituting of the older ones.

Note should be taken, however, of insight into this question that is available from another source: namely, the history of state boards of education for the overall supervision of public elementary and secondary education. These agencies, present in all the states (although in Illinois and Wisconsin the state boards deal only with vocational education, and the superintendent of public instruction and state department of education oversee the other aspects of the public school program) have duties and powers with respect to the lower schools much like those of statewide coordinating boards over public higher education. The state boards of education are overwhelmingly composed of lay persons, appointed to office by the

---

20 *Ibid.*, pp. 91-155.
21 Kentucky Revised Statutes, Section 164.010, 1962.
22 Glenny, *op. cit.*
23 Chambers, *op. cit.*

governor to represent the interests of the people of the state at large.[24]

Speaking before the Association of Governing Boards of State Universities and Allied Institutions, this writer traced the comparison of statewide boards for public education further, stating as a conclusion:

> The point to be noted in all this is the commitment to the principle of local control within a system of statewide supervision and coordination. This is what makes the American system of education unique among those of the world, the staunch observance of control by local boards of trustees of lay citizens within the general statewide structure of public education. Dr. Hollis and I see in the analysis we made of 209 state boards responsible for higher education a drift toward the same structure in higher education.[25]

Evidences of progress toward the ideal. The proposition that both institutional autonomy and interinstitutional coordination and planning are essential for a system of colleges and universities to operate successfully in accomplishing the total educational purposes of the system is steadily gaining acceptance. This is evident both in the development of new practices and procedures in administering higher institutions and in the statements of leaders in research and practice in the field.

The practice already described in this monograph of preserving and even strengthening institutional boards of trustees while creating mechanisms for system-wide coordination of institutions of higher learning is on the increase. Although strongest in evidence among the state-supported networks of colleges and universities (in 1962 such a structure was found in ten states), the use of both institutional boards and an overall coordinating body is emerging in the realm of privately controlled higher education where groups of institutions have some common purposes to their programs. Thus, for example, the Board of Higher Education of the Methodist Church; the Education Commission of the Southern Baptist Convention; the Board of

---

[24] Fred F. Beach and Robert F. Will, *The State and Education: The Structure and Control of Public Education at the State Level,* U.S. Office of Education (Washington, D.C.: USGPO, 1955), pp. 7-12.

[25] S. V. Martorana, "State Boards Responsible for Higher Education," in *Proceedings,* Association of Governing Boards of State Universities and Allied Institutions, October 19-22, 1960 (Denver, Colo.: Association of Governing Boards, 1961), pp. 66-72.

Higher Education of the Church of Jesus Christ of the Latter Day Saints; and the office of the President, Jesuit Educational Association of the Society of Jesus of the Roman Catholic Church; perform significant duties of interinstitutional coordination among the colleges affiliated with these organizations.

Emphatic assertion and constant reiteration of the validity of the concept stated above is found in the literature. Notions as to the best way to implement the idea differ, but the basic concept has wide support, as indicated in all of the plans for coordination described by McConnell [26] in arriving at his suggested "general plan." The main item of debate has been noted to center not on the concept itself, but on the extent to which the coordination should be "voluntary" and the structure to accomplish the program directly representative of the colleges and universities involved.

The use of a professionally trained specialist to serve as the chief executive officer of the board and as supporting workers to him is historically well-established in college administration. As boards have developed to set policies and to coordinate groups of colleges and universities, they also have come to rely on the aid of professionally trained specialists. As yet the chief executive officer of statewide coordinating boards, designated variously as "chancellor," "executive director," or "executive secretary," evidently has not achieved a professional status comparable to that of the chief executive officer of institutional boards of trustees, the college or university president.[27] Perhaps this can also be claimed as true of the relative position of professional personnel in central offices of the networks of privately controlled higher institutions. There appears to be little reason, however, to think that the use of professional specialists by all types of boards of higher education will be diminished.

"Higher education in America must be pluralistic, not monolithic," states M. M. Chambers.[28] To this may be added that higher educational institutions in America must ever be sensitive to changes in the social, economic, and cultural setting and in the services expected of them. The structure for administration of higher educa-

---

[26] McConnell, *op. cit.*, pp. 136-52.

[27] Martorana and Hollis, *op. cit.*, p. 39.

[28] M. M. Chambers, *The Campus and the People* (Danville, Ill.: The Interstate Printers and Publishers, Inc., 1960), p. 26.

tion that has evolved in this country to attain effectively both these goals entails a fundamental reliance on boards of trustees made up of laymen and their staffs of professionally trained personnel. Trustees, to do their tasks well, need to know what the board on which they hold membership is responsible for and how to build and utilize a competent professional staff. And they must be constantly aware of the exceedingly great trust that has been placed in them by the constituencies of the colleges and universities of the nation.

Bibliography

Association of Governing Boards of State Universities and Allied Institutions, *Proceedings*. 38th Annual Meeting, Seattle, Washington, October 19–22, 1960. Denver, Colo.: Association of Governing Boards, 1961. 129 pp.

————, *Proceedings*. 39th Annual Meeting, Lincoln, Nebraska, October 10–14, 1961. Denver, Colo.: Association of Governing Boards, 1962. 159 pp.

Beach, Fred F., and Robert F. Will, *The State and Education*. U.S. Office of Education, Misc. No. 23. Washington, D.C.: USGPO, 1955. viii, 175 pp.

————, *The State and Nonpublic Schools*. U.S. Office of Education, Misc. No. 28. Washington, D.C.: USGPO, 1958. vii, 152 pp.

Beck, Hubert Park, *Men Who Control Our Universities: The Economic and Social Composition of Governing Boards of Thirty Leading American Universities*. New York: King's Crown Press, 1947. ix, 229 pp.

Belcher, Donald R., *The Board of Trustees of the University of Pennsylvania*. Philadelphia: University of Pennsylvania Press, 1960. 112 pp.

Blackwell, Thomas E., *College Law—A Guide for Administrators*. Washington, D.C.: American Council on Education, 1961. ix, 347 pp.

Burns, Gerald P., ed., *Administrators in Higher Education—Their Functions and Coordination*. New York: Harper & Row, Publishers, 1962. xii, 236 pp.

Capen, Samuel P., *The Management of Universities*. Buffalo, N.Y.: Foster and Stewart Publishing Company, 1953. xii, 288 pp.

Chambers, M. M., *The Campus and the People: Organization, Support and Control of Higher Education in the United States in the Nineteen Sixties*. Danville, Ill.: The Interstate Printers and Publishers, Inc., 1960. iv, 75 pp.

————, *Voluntary Statewide Coordination in Public Higher Education*. Ann Arbor, Mich.: The University of Michigan Press, 1961. xi, 83 pp.

Corson, John J., *Governance of Colleges and Universities*. New York: McGraw-Hill Book Company, 1960. vi, 209 pp.

Deferrari, Roy J., ed., *College Organization and Administration*. The Proceedings of the Workshop on College Organization and Administration, conducted at The Catholic University of America, June 17–27, 1946. Washington, D.C.: The Catholic University of America Press, 1947. 403 pp.

————, *The Problems of Administration in the American College*. The Proceedings of the Workshop on Problems of Administration in the American College conducted at The Catholic University of America, June 10–12, 1955. Washington, D.C.: The Catholic University of America Press, 1956. vii, 191 pp.

Dodds, Harold W., *The Academic President—Educator or Caretaker?* New York: McGraw-Hill Book Company, 1962. ix, 294 pp.

Eells, Walter Crosby, "Boards of Control of Universities and Colleges," *The Educational Record*, XLII (October, 1961), 336–42.

Elliott, Edward C., M. M. Chambers, and William A. Ashbrook, *The Government of Higher Education*. New York: American Book Company, 1935. xiv, 289 pp.

Geier, Woodrow A., ed., *Effective Trustees, A Report*. National Conference of Trustees for Church Colleges at Lake Junaluska, North Carolina, June 26–28, 1959. Nashville, Tenn.: Division of Educational Institutions, Board of Education, The Methodist Church, 1959, 100 pp.

Glenny, Lyman A., *Autonomy of Public Colleges, The Challenge of Coordination*. New York: McGraw-Hill Book Company, 1959. xix, 325 pp.

Hofstadter, Richard, and Wilson Smith, eds., *American Higher Education, A Documentary History*. 2 volumes. Chicago: The University of Chicago Press, 1961. xv, 1016 pp.

Hughes, Raymond M., *A Manual for Trustees of Colleges and Universities*. Ames, Iowa: The Iowa State College Press, 1943. ix, 166 pp.

McConnell, T. R., *A General Pattern for American Public Higher Education*. New York: McGraw-Hill Book Company, 1962. xi, 198 pp.

Martorana, S. V., and Ernest V. Hollis, *State Boards Responsible for Higher Education*. U.S. Office of Education, Circular No. 619. Washington, D.C.: USGPO, 1960. x, 254 pp.

Moos, Malcolm, and Francis E. Rourke, *The Campus and the State*. Baltimore, Md.: The Johns Hopkins Press, 1959. xii, 414 pp.

Nielsen, Oswald, ed., *University Administration in Practice*. Stanford, Calif.: Stanford University Graduate School of Business, 1959. viii, 168 pp.

Quinlivan, Ray J., "President's Address," in Association of Governing Boards of State Universities and Allied Institutions, *Proceedings*, 1953, pp. 24–30. Denver, Colo.: Association of Governing Boards, 1954.

Rauh, Morton, *College and University Trusteeship*. Yellow Springs, Ohio: The Antioch Press, 1959. 112 pp.

Ruml, Beardsley, and Donald H. Morrison, *Memo to a College Trustee: A Report on Financial and Structural Problems of the Liberal College*. New York: McGraw-Hill Book Company, 1959. xiv, 94 pp.

Russell, John Dale, *Higher Education in Michigan*. The final report of the survey of higher education in Michigan, prepared for the Michigan Legislative Study Committee on Higher Education, September, 1958. Lansing, Mich.: Legislative Study Committee on Higher Education, 1958. xvii, 185 pp.

————,*The Finance of Higher Education*, rev. ed. Chicago: University of Chicago Press, 1954. xix, 416 pp.

Russell, John Dale, and Floyd W. Reeves, *The Evaluation of Higher Institutions*, Vol. VI: *Administration*. A series of monographs based on the investigation conducted for the committee on revision of standards, Commission on Higher Institutions of the North Central Association of Colleges and Secondary Schools. Chicago: The University of Chicago Press, 1936. xx, 285 pp.

Wilson, Logan, *The Academic Man, A Study in the Sociology of a Profession*. New York: Oxford University Press, 1942. viii, 248 pp.

Index

Index